Alber

Titles in the series Critical Lives present the work of leading cultural figures of the modern period. Each book explores the life of the artist, writer, philosopher or architect in question and relates it to their major works.

In the same series

Albert Camus

Edward J. Hughes

REAKTION BOOKS

*This book is fondly dedicated to the memory of
Rory Hamilton, 1952–2012*

Published by Reaktion Books Ltd
33 Great Sutton Street
London EC1V 0DX, UK
www.reaktionbooks.co.uk

First published 2015
Copyright © Edward J. Hughes 2015

Printed and bound in Great Britain
by Bell & Bain, Glasgow

A catalogue record for this book is available from the British Library

ISBN 978 1 78023 493 9

Contents

Note on Texts, Abbreviations and Translations

References to Camus' works are made using the following abbreviations:

CAC   *Camus à 'Combat'*, ed. Jacqueline Lévi-Valensi (Paris, 2002)

EK   Albert Camus, *Exile and the Kingdom*, trans. Carol Cosman (London, 2013)

FM   Albert Camus, *The First Man*, trans. David Hapgood (London, 1995)

OC   Albert Camus, *Œuvres complètes*, 4 vols (Paris, 2006–8), ed. Jacqueline Lévi-Valensi (vols I and II) and Raymond Gay-Crosier (vols III and IV)

Where printed English translations are used, these are indicated. All other translations are my own.

Albert Camus, photographed for *Vogue* by Cecil Beaton, New York, 1946.

Introduction: 'Who is Camus?'

Once the 'commotion', as he described it, of his Nobel Prize for Literature in 1957 had begun to subside, Albert Camus wrote to his primary school teacher back in Algiers, Louis Germain, to express his sense of gratitude: 'my first thought, after my mother, was of you', he confessed in an open expression of gratitude from someone who 'despite the years, has never stopped being your grateful pupil. I embrace you with all my heart' (*FM*, 257). The sentimental style (Camus saw in Germain a father-figure) is reciprocated in a letter Germain wrote to Camus on 30 April 1959. Germain had fought in the First World War and the knowledge that Camus was one of the orphans of that conflict (Lucien Camus, his father, had died, aged 29, on 11 October 1914 from wounds received at the Battle of the Marne) had triggered in Germain a paternal interest in the progress of his talented pupil. Camus recalls the end-of-term ritual for the class of ten-year-old boys at the *école communale* in rue Aumerat in French colonial Algiers when Germain would read, with such conviction and empathy, from Roland Dorgelès' patriotic novel about life in the trenches, *Les Croix de bois* (The Wooden Crosses, 1919).

This was 1923–4 and talk of the First World War was part of the world in which Camus and his classmates grew up. Indeed he remarked that in those early years they heard about nothing else. As an adolescent, he would visit a home for disabled ex-service-men, the Maison des Invalides in Kouba in the pleasant Sahel

countryside at the end of the tram line to the east of Algiers, travelling with a schoolfriend whose mother worked in the laundry
there. After the initial shock, the sight of the war amputees, many
of them young men, became normal for the adolescent Camus
(*FM*, 185–90).

The state education system was one of the ideological mainstays
of the Third French Republic, which vaunted the educative and
social role of the primary school teacher: the *instituteur* was to be a
vital transmitter of French cultural values. As his letter of gratitude
to Germain demonstrates, Camus' case provides an eloquent illus-
tration of this. That said, in his congratulatory letter to Camus of
April 1959, Germain does not claim to know everything about his
pupil-turned-public-figure:

> Who is Camus? I have the impression that those who try to
> penetrate your nature do not quite succeed. You have always
> shown an instinctive reticence about revealing your nature, your
> feelings. You succeed all the more for being unaffected, direct.[1]

Who indeed was Camus? In a logbook published as the conclusion
to a collection of essays entitled *L'Eté* (Summer), he writes with a
mixture of aloofness and insecurity of walking along fashionable
streets and receiving praise from passers-by who ask him who he is.
The reply comes back: 'Nothing yet, nothing yet . . .' (*OC*, III, 616).
The same logbook opens with a wistful evocation of Camus' Algiers
boyhood: 'I grew up in the sea and for me poverty was sumptuous
but then I lost the sea; luxury in all its forms seemed grey to me
and life's misery intolerable. Since then I have been waiting.'
Camus had crossed the Atlantic to New York in March 1946 and
undertook another long crossing, from Marseilles to Rio de
Janeiro, when he visited Brazil in the summer of 1949: memories of
the sea journeys fed into this text composed in 1953.[2] In the moody
self-portrait, the sense of disarray and evasiveness is striking in a

writer with his trademark Humphrey Bogart looks who had an established reputation as the author of *L'Etranger* (The Outsider, 1942) and *La Peste* (The Plague, 1947) and who had covered the Liberation of Paris and the end of the Second World War as a high-profile national journalist. While controversies to do with the Cold War and colonial Algeria ensured that Camus remained very much a public figure in the 1950s, a no less sombre mood marks a diary entry for 2 August 1958 in which he reflects that he forced himself to keep this written record even though he found it repugnant:

> for me, life is secret. It is secret in relation to others . . . but it must also be so in my own eyes, I should not reveal it in words. Muted and unformulated, that is how life is rich for me (*oc*, IV, 1285).

The suspicion directed against the verbal articulation of feeling forms a striking element in this psychological self-portrait and gives weight to Louis Germain's question about who his former pupil might be. Camus' one-time friend and later adversary Jean-Paul Sartre, writing a few days after Camus' premature death in January 1960, looked back on the life of a writer 'on the move [who] questioned and challenged us, who was himself a question that was seeking its answer'.[3]

In the last year of his life, Camus had focused substantially on what was to remain his unfinished novel *Le Premier Homme* (The First Man), describing the work as a welcome turn in his writing towards those he loved. The context was crucial. By that stage, Algeria was over four years into a war that would eventually lead to the independence of the country in 1962. Camus was intensely aware of the increasing isolation of the European Algerian tribe to which he belonged.

Within Algeria's indigenous Berber and Arab populations, which numbered eight million in the 1950s, against one million

European Algerians, there was radical discontent long before the outbreak of the War of Independence in November 1954. The events of Sétif in May 1945 (when French retaliation against the Algerian killing of over a hundred Europeans led to thousands of Muslim deaths) had radicalized many Algerians.[4] The events in Philippeville in the Constantine region in August 1955 saw a repeat of attacks on European civilians followed by brutal French military reprisals causing thousands of Muslim casualties. Philippeville became a watershed moment in the conflict. In metropolitan France, the effect of the escalation of the war with the Battle of Algiers in the first half of 1957, when the French army occupied the Casbah, was to convince increasing numbers that negotiation with the Algerian rebels was the only way forward.[5]

Algeria also triggered in 1958 the return to power of Charles de Gaulle, who sought a way out of a conflict that was weakening France's global position. He announced on 16 September 1959 the right of Algerians to self-determination. If the negative perception of French Algerian attitudes in progressive liberal circles in France left Camus increasingly isolated during the Algerian War, he insisted in *The First Man* that those he referred to as his own had themselves often been marginalized by European history: working-class Parisians expelled from France after the political violence that came with the 1848 Revolution and European economic migrants encouraged to settle in Algeria by France as she sought to consolidate her colonial occupation of Algeria. The Franco–Prussian War of 1870–71 had also seen many French fleeing Alsace-Lorraine after the Prussian annexation of the provinces. These victims of France's defeat, the persecuted, as Camus put it, went on to become persecutors, he reflected, by settling on Algerian land from which native Berbers had been expelled when the French quelled a major indigenous rebellion in 1871 (*FM*, 149).[6]

Camus' life thus came to be inextricably tied up with the fluctuating fortunes of French colonial rule in Algeria. He conceded that

Monument to the Dead of the First World War, Algiers. Camus would write in 1950:
'I grew up, like all those of my generation, to the sound of the drums of the First
World War and our history since then has been nothing but one of murder,
injustice, violence' (*oc*, III, 606).

the country's working-class European settlers were culturally inward-looking and he castigated wealthy colonialists for their greedy preservation of economic and political supremacy. Moreover, he was under no illusions about French Algeria's right-wing political orientation in the decades after the First World War, with its endorsement of the reactionary French nationalism of Charles Maurras, its backing for Franco's dictatorship in Spain and its culture of anti-Semitism.

Camus' own political alignment was left-wing although he disliked being pigeonholed. As he remarked to a group of international students in Aix-en-Provence shortly before he died, his allegiance was to the Left, in spite of himself and in spite of the Left.[7] On the question of the French presence in Algeria, he was outspoken about the social and economic deprivation inflicted on the Arab and Berber populations of the country by the colonial regime. But he remained French Algerian in his outlook, continuing to believe in the feasibility of Franco-Algerian coexistence and categorically refusing to endorse calls for Algerian independence in the late 1950s.

If the connection to Algeria was strong, Camus was also intensely conscious of being a product of his age. Mindful of his generation's exposure to a legacy of global violence, he saw this as leaving little room for optimism and indeed in many cases as spawning a culture of nihilism.[8] Speaking at the University of Uppsala a few days after receiving his Nobel Prize, he recalled the case of the ancient Chinese sage whose regular prayer was to be spared from living in 'interesting times' (*oc*, IV, 247), a euphemism for a time of conflict. 'The most terrible century in Western history' ensured there was to be no such avoidance of conflict for Camus and his generation.[9] As a creator of fiction, a playwright, a journalist and public commentator, he wrote against a backdrop dominated by world conflict and the fall of empire. He referred to 'all the errors, contradictions and hesitations' (*oc*, IV, 304) that had marked his involvement with Algeria. But as one critic has observed, it is not 'a matter of espousing or rejecting' Camus' position but of understanding the historical context which shaped it.[10] Camus' achievements and limitations and the impasses he encountered along the way are the subject of the chapters that follow.

1

Literacy, or 'the Regular Rows of the Lines'[1]

Albert Camus was born on 7 November 1913. He was descended from nineteenth-century, working-class European settlers in colonial Algeria. The French had been there since 1830 when a naval bombardment of the port of Algiers signalled the beginning of a military conquest of the country. His birthplace was a village named Saint-Paul near Mondovi in the Constantine region of eastern Algeria where the family had moved earlier that year from Algiers, his father Lucien Camus working as an agricultural labourer for a wine-producing company, Ricôme. By the time of Camus' first birthday, the family had moved back to Algiers and, having lost the head of the household in the war, was living in hard times in a working-class district in the eastern half of the city.

In *The First Man*, his largely autobiographical and unfinished work which was published posthumously in 1994, Camus makes much of the feet-on-the-ground ordinariness of Algeria's European community, which was made up predominantly of French settlers but also included migrants from Italy, Spain, Malta and elsewhere. The Camus family reflected this mix, with his father's side coming originally from France, while his mother Catherine Sintès was descended from Spanish migrants. The horizons of the working-class settlers were dominated by narrow considerations of economic need and in the case of his own family, Camus identifies what he terms in *The First Man* 'the awful wear and tear of poverty' (*FM*, 128).

As he makes clear in that work, however, there were degrees of poverty in colonial Algeria and his family's situation did not come close to the destitution experienced by the country's Berber and Arab populations. Thus the narrator in *The First Man* records how, in a street near the local market in the Belcourt district of Algiers where he grew up, the rubbish was regularly rummaged through by those who were most deprived:

> famished Arabs or Moors, or sometimes an old Spanish tramp, had pried open [dustbins] at dawn to see if there was still something to be retrieved from what poor and thrifty families had so disdained they would throw it away (*FM*, 108).

Income discrepancies across ethnicities were perennially stark in the colony, with the earnings of a European Algerian estimated to be 28 times those of an Algerian Muslim in the 1950s. A French government-sponsored report in 1955 showed that 93 per cent of Algerian Muslims belonged to the poorest section of society.[2]

The economic hardship facing working-class settlers such as the Camus family was nevertheless real and set them apart from the colonial bourgeoisie. Camus reflects dryly on the task facing the priest responsible for preparing for First Communion the 'rough, obdurate children' (*FM*, 132) of this simple people, or *'petit peuple'*. Anticlericalism was widespread within the working-class descendants of nineteenth-century French colonizers and any adherence to Catholic ritual in Camus' family when he was growing up was minimal.

Schooling, by contrast, was deeply formative for Camus and his early exposure to the French educational system and subsequent career as a journalist and writer, firstly in Algiers and then in Paris, were to take him a considerable way from his working-class roots in colonial North Africa. His family embodied, unexceptionally, the culture of manual labour typical of the Belcourt district on the east side of Algiers. His mother worked as a domestic and his maternal uncle Etienne Sintès was a barrel-maker in a small local factory. The autobiographical *The First Man* describes how on Thursdays when school was closed, the boy Jacques Cormery would rush his homework so as to get down to the cooperage and experience the world of manual work (*FM*, 96–9). Camus was regularly outspoken about capitalism's economic exploitation of the working class but he was also attracted to the materiality of manual labour. In one of his short stories of the 1950s, 'Les Muets' (The Silent Ones), the barrel-maker Yvars, although bitterly frustrated with his employer, nevertheless feels a release from tension through the sensory experience of working with wood. Planing a piece of timber, '[Yvars] recognized the old familiar smell and the tension in his heart eased a bit' (*OC*, IV, 39). The developed sensuality in Camus translates into Yvars' sentient awareness.

Home life for the young Camus unfolded within an atmosphere of inarticulacy and frequent silence. His mother Catherine Sintès, had severe hearing difficulties contracted as a result of sickness as a child (*FM*, 63). Her oral communication was limited. Moreover, the adult family members were illiterate in contrast to the two boys, Albert and his older brother Lucien. In an emotional protest against its injustice, Camus evokes the life of social exclusion and physical toil lived by his mother. He notes the

> invisible barrier behind which for all his life he had seen her take shelter – gentle, polite, complaisant, even passive, and yet never conquered by anyone or anything, isolated by her semi-deafness, her difficulty in expressing herself, beautiful surely but virtually inaccessible (*FM*, 46).

Catherine Sintès remained a widow after losing her husband in the war in 1914:

washing floors on her knees, living without a man and without solace in the midst of the greasy leavings and dirty linen of other people's lives, the long days of labour adding up one by one to a life that, by dint of being deprived of hope, had become also a life without any sort of resentment, unaware, persevering, a life resigned to all kinds of suffering, her own as well as that of others (*FM*, 46).

She was unable to hear the radio or to read the newspaper, of which the illustrations were the only part which had any meaning for her. Her silent observation was instead directed to the life of Belcourt in the street below, 'the same street that she had been contemplating through half her lifetime' (*FM*, 76). Her brother Etienne, who shared the cramped family home in the rue de Lyon (now the rue Belouizdad), was also partially deaf and had a vocabulary of about a hundred words (*FM*, 77). If we continue to mine *The First Man* for its biographical information, we see that decades later Camus, back from France on a family visit to Algiers, found his mother and uncle living together in a mutually supportive way, 'carrying on a mute dialogue lit up from time to time by scraps of sentences, but more connected and better informed about each other than many normal couples' (*FM*, 100). The image of largely silent bonding between ageing siblings shows Camus entirely at ease with this particular style of cohabitation. On a visit to the author's family home in Algiers in March 1948, the novelist Louis Guilloux was struck by the largely silent interaction between Camus and his mother. This atypical experience was to feed into his fiction, where minimal verbal communication forms a leitmotif.

Camus was already an established author by the time he came to know more about his father. Lucien Camus was himself someone of reportedly few words, the writer learns from a past work associate who vaguely remembers a taciturn figure: '"No talker, he was no talker"' (*FM*, 144). These private lives and precarious memories assume wider cultural and in a sense political ramifications in Camus' late work as they come to be mapped onto an anxiety about France's place in Algeria in the mid- to late 1950s. A diary entry of 29 July 1958 shows Camus seized with panic: 'In the morning I am obsessed by Algeria. Too late, too late . . . If my homeland were to be lost, I would no longer be worth anything' (*OC*, IV, 1284). In *The First Man*, he was giving voice to the insecurity arising from the son's memory of his father disappearing 'behind this immense and hostile land . . . into the anonymous history of the village and the plain' (*FM*, 145).

In Camus' boyhood, it was his maternal grandmother Catherine-Maria Sintès (née Cardona) born in 1857 in the village of San Luis on the Spanish island of Menorca, who ruled the roost. His widowed mother remained submissive to the imposing figure of her own mother who had lost many of her family to premature death. 'She was as familiar with death as she was with work or poverty', we read in *The First Man*. Indeed the material pressures of everyday living were to leave his grandmother and many others in Algeria, Camus writes, indifferent to 'the funerary piety that flourishes in civilizations at their height' (*FM*, 128).

Postcard of the Théâtre Municipal and Place de la République, early 20th-century Algiers.

The popular quarter of Bab-el-Oued in Algiers, close to where Camus attended the Grand Lycée.

The cultural narrowness of home life came into sharp focus for the young Camus when, just before his eleventh birthday, he took the tram to the other side of Algiers to begin secondary school at the main French lycée situated near the Bab-el-Oued district of the city and close to the Casbah. Home life in Belcourt meant cultural restriction: 'Neither the images, nor things written, nor word of mouth, nor the veneer of culture acquired in everyday conversation had reached them' (*FM*, 158). The intervention of Louis Germain, the inspirational primary school teacher singled out by Camus when he won the Nobel Prize, was pivotal in ensuring the transition to secondary school. Germain acted as a tactful intermediary between the world of formal education and Camus' family. Seeing his pupil's talent and convinced that he should go to the lycée, he visited the family home to explain to Camus' mother and grandmother how the transfer from the *école communale* worked. He gave Camus and other boys extra tuition as they prepared for the entrance examinations and he accompanied them across the city to the lycée on the day of the entrance tests.

A culture clash awaited Germain's pupils at the lycée. Throughout his life, Camus was never to feel wholly at ease with the cultural baggage that he acquired through the French school system and beyond.[3] In his case, to talk about family at the lycée often required a form of cultural translation, so atypical was his background. Yet where he did not stand out, Camus noted, was in the matter of his father's death in the First World War. This meant that, like his older brother Lucien, he was one of the many 'pupilles de la nation', children placed under the guardianship of a nation that recognized the sacrifice made by its war dead. The lycée served a significant role in French colonial culture, acting as a powerful conduit for metropolitan French values. In the case of Camus' school, a roll of the drums would punctuate the different parts of the school day (as his philosophy teacher Jean Grenier would later confess to Camus, it was that display of regimentation which drove him out of Algiers).[4]

Much more pronounced in Algerian society than class differences, the narrator reflects in *The First Man*, were differences of race. At primary school, the European Algerians might have had some Muslim classmates whereas at the lycée it was only in exceptional cases that Muslim pupils attended. The school canteen staff, Camus notes, were Arab, to use the designation routinely adopted by Europeans of his day. The name of the main lycée in Algiers itself reflected the country's colonial history. When Camus started there in 1924, it was the Grand Lycée d'Alger. It was to be renamed the Lycée Bugeaud at the time of the centenary celebration of French colonial rule in Algeria in 1930 (Bugeaud had led the bloody military conquest of Algeria in the 1840s). And with Algerian independence in 1962, it was to become the Lycée Abd-el-Kader in memory of one of Algeria's most prominent military figures, who had waged *jihad* against the French in Algeria in the 1830s and '40s.

Life at the lycée introduced Camus to a bourgeois world in which his own social origins contrasted markedly with those of many of his fellow pupils. Needing to complete a school form which requested information about parental occupations, he had put down that his mother was a 'ménagère' when a classmate – also from working-class Belcourt and whose mother worked for the Post Office – explained that the term 'ménagère' designated a woman who looked after her own home. The category needed was, apparently, 'domestique' and Camus' autobiographical hero Jacques Cormery feels not only the strangeness of this term but shame both at using it and at his own reaction of shame (*FM*, 159). The requirement of a parental signature on a school form was no less problematic, for even though his mother had by that stage learnt how to sign for her war widow's pension, there was no one else at home able to sign in her absence, a fact that did not go unnoticed at school (*FM*, 161).

The power-play around language and access to the printed word which were to become prominent themes in Camus' fictional world thus have their basis in his early experience of family life. For the young schoolboy, home was a world without newspapers and radio, where there were no books but only 'objects of immediate utility, where no one but relatives visited, a home they rarely left and then only to meet other members of the same ignorant family' (*FM*, 158). The clear sense is of an enclosed, culturally limited world.

Years later, when the adult son, by then a high-profile writer in Paris, travelled back to visit his mother, the only objects that he found aside from the basic furniture were a copper ashtray of Arabic design (left out for his use) and a standard-issue French Post Office calendar (*FM*, 48). The returning son was similarly struck by the sight of a kitchen dresser still containing, as before, only the bare minimum of food: 'its nakedness fascinated him' (*FM*, 47). Camus, again through the character of Jacques Cormery, reflects on how he had grown up in a family milieu without paintings or other forms of decoration, and how when he later spent time in the homes of the better-off, the contrast was striking.

Camus was still at primary school when in 1921 his family moved into a three-room flat at 93 rue de Lyon, having previously lived at number seventeen. The part of the street they were now in was in the district of Belcourt where Catherine Sintès had begun her married life. Space at number 93 was limited, with Camus and his older brother and mother sharing a bedroom, his grandmother in a second bedroom and his Uncle Etienne sleeping in the kitchen.[5] In December 1930, Camus, aged seventeen, was diagnosed with tuberculosis. Then a prevalent disease in the West with often fatal consequences, it caused serious disruption to his studies at the lycée. The illness was to recur at numerous times in his life and put paid in the medium term to his hopes of becoming a teacher of philosophy: in the autumn of 1938 he failed a medical which ruled out his taking the *agrégation*, France's national competition for the annual recruitment of high-achieving teachers.

As part of his convalescence, the seventeen-year-old Camus lived for a while in the home of a prosperous uncle, Gustave Acault. Acault's butcher's premises on the rue Michelet (now the rue Didouche-Mourad) sold meat imported from France to the middle-class *Français de France* (French from France) who were unimpressed by the quality of what was produced locally.[6] Acault was married to Catherine Camus' sister, Antoinette. Camus later described him as attending to his business in the morning and spending the rest of the day in his well-stocked library or in cafés discussing ideas (*oc*, III, 881).

A key marker of the class and people Camus belonged to, he noted, came via language. When growing up at home, the designation of everyday objects was plain: the vase on the mantelpiece, the pot, the soup dishes (*FM*, 48). He was to discover a different view of material culture across town in the Acaults' house, where they would talk about the Vosges earthenware or the Quimper dinner service: 'Jacques had grown up in the midst of a poverty naked as death, among things named with common nouns; it was at his uncle's that he discovered those proper nouns' (*FM*, 48).

The reflection around language continued to energize Camus the writer as he looked back on his early family life. He recalled with nostalgia visits to the municipal library on Thursdays when school was closed and he evoked the escapism that came with the reading of the cloak-and-dagger *Pardaillan* novels by the writer Michel Zévaco (*FM*, 190–91). Camus noted how around the time he started in the lycée – this would have been in the mid-1920s – a municipal library had been built on the border between the dusty streets of Belcourt and the more fashionable residences which began near the Parc Sainte-Odile, with small gardens in which plants thrived in the humid conditions of Algiers: 'Villas stretched along one bank of this frontier and low-cost buildings along the other' (*FM*, 191). The class divide within the European settler community was itself marked.

Over an extended period of time spent reading fiction, the young Camus and a lycée friend from the neighbourhood enjoyed this access to

a whole universe of images and memories that never yielded to the reality of their daily lives, and that surely was no less immediate to these eager children who lived their dreams as intensely as they did their lives (*FM*, 192).

The exposure to literature was thus keenly lived by the future writer. *The First Man* reconstructs this: merely entering the space of the library took the boy out of the 'dusty and treeless' (*FM*, 191) world of Belcourt and he would rush home with the standard library issue of two books, settling down to read them by the light of an oil lamp falling on the cheap waxed tablecloth. The crude composition of the fiction did not dent the boy's pleasure, just as long as the action was violent and clearly described.

That the mother of this avid young reader was herself illiterate was to add to the complex emotional relationship between them. In *The First Man*, Camus evokes a curious moment when the hero's mother is intrigued by the world of reading. Like her son, she too smells the book but there the parallel ends:

> 'It's the library', she would say. She mispronounced this word she had heard spoken by her son that had no meaning to her, but she recognized the jackets of books. 'Yes', Jacques said without looking up. Catherine Cormery leaned over his shoulder. She looked at the double rectangle under the light, the regular rows of the lines; she would inhale the odour, and sometimes she would run her swollen fingers, wrinkled by the water from doing laundry, across the page, as if she were trying better to understand what a book was, to come a little closer to these mysterious signs, incomprehensible to her, but where her son so often and for hours on end found a life unknown to her and from which he would return with such an expression, looking at her as if she were a stranger (*FM*, 194).

The phenomenon of the printed book intrigues the son and his mother, the one participating actively as an eager consumer of fiction, the other a bemused onlooker unable to enter the space of reading. Fiction is both available and absent and the contrast triggers emotional confusion: the mother appears to look in on the mystery of 'the double rectangle under the light, the regular rows of the lines', and she seems alien in the eyes of her son as he re-emerges from reading. With access to books awakening these contrasting responses, literature as a chosen pathway in life risked becoming for Camus a form of betrayal, a disengagement from family origins. His career as a writer based for many years in Paris was to take him far from the world of domestic and factory labour that was the life experience of other members of his family. Yet he never became a Parisian insider. Nor did the high profile that came with being a Gallimard author spell divorce from his origins. Yet the emotional tension which came with that career trajectory is reflected in Camus' choice of dedicatee for *The First Man*: 'To you who will never be able to read this book' – the 'you' being his mother, '[the] Widow Camus' (*FM*, 3).

Shuttling between these two worlds was to play a pivotal role in Camus' writing project. As a secondary school pupil, he would travel across town by tram each day to the terminus at Place du Gouvernement. From there he and his Belcourt classmate would make their way to the lycée near the busy rue Bab-Azoun with its arcades (*FM*, 167). A typical day saw Camus spend twelve hours there, living 'to the sound of the drum, in a society of children and teachers, amidst games and study' (*FM*, 195). Coming from a poor background, he was a day-boarder with extended access to school facilities, including entitlement to school meals, starting with breakfast at 7.15 am. The very full day meant no more than two or three hours each evening back home with his mother 'whom he did not really join except in the sleep of the poor' (*FM*, 195) – this a reference to the bedroom Catherine Camus shared with her two sons. Thus while working-class Belcourt lay at the heart of Camus' early experience of life, the long lycée days meant that for the adolescent his neighbourhood came to be associated with night, sleep and dreams (*FM*, 195).

With the stark divide between home and school, life at the Grand Lycée did not feature in family conversation, nor did any of its pupils or teachers ever come to Camus' home. The exception was when, quite late on in his schooling, Jean Grenier turned up to visit his sick pupil. Grenier was from Brittany and was to become an author with the Paris publishing house Gallimard. He was surprised to see the conditions in which Camus' family lived and he remembered how on the occasion of that visit, his pupil was stand-offish, speaking only in monosyllables. 'In your eyes', Grenier wrote in 1942, 'I represented SOCIETY but for me you have never been "the Outsider" [L'Étranger]'. He was referring to Camus' first novel, which had appeared a few months earlier.[7]

Looking back on the annual prize-giving at the lycée, the adult Camus recalled going along with his nervous mother and grandmother, both of them in their Sunday best with the grandmother, embarrassingly for the boy, wearing a black mantilla as Spanish women of her generation did (FM, 197). The ceremony was an occasion to showcase Frenchness in the colonial city that was Algiers, with a military band getting things under way with a rendition of the Marseillaise at two in the afternoon and the task of delivering the 'discours solennel', or solemn academic address, falling traditionally to the youngest teacher, usually recently graduated in France, who would lace his speech with learned humanist allusions that were lost on the European Algerian audience. Unsurprisingly, this atmosphere of patriotic fervour and scholarly pretention washed over Camus' mother if we are to go by the mocking evocation to be found in The First Man, where Catherine Cormery 'received without blinking the rain of erudition and wisdom that was falling on her without interruption' (FM, 198). Back home, with the visit to the lycée over for another year, she would change into her normal clothes and resume sitting passively by the window which looked out on to Belcourt below.

But for the young Camus, as the historians Benjamin Stora and Jean-Baptiste Péretié underline, primary school and the lycée were key in shaping his sense of French republican values.[8] Indeed Camus was to appeal to the values of fraternity and equality when campaigning vigorously in the late 1930s and beyond for economic and social reform for the country's majority-Muslim population. Yet as we will see, his reformist campaigning in the 1930s and '40s was to lose traction in the 1950s with the country's majority demanding independence.[9]

2

'True Love . . . Awkward Pages'

Like Louis Germain before him, Jean Grenier (whom Camus
would later refer to as 'le bon maître', or the wise old master)
played a major role in Camus' development.[1] He suggested his
pupil read two novels in particular by authors whom Grenier
knew personally. André de Richaud's *La Douleur* (Grief, 1930),
the story of a First World War widow and her life of social margin-
alization, allowed the young Camus to see that the compass of
literature could take in the world of poverty. And Louis Guilloux's
La Maison du peuple (The House of the People, 1927), provided
another account of poverty, this time affecting a cobbler and his
family in Saint-Brieuc in pre-1914 Brittany. Guilloux's novel evokes
the attempt by workers to combat class exploitation and his
sympathetic account of social struggle struck a chord with Camus.
In the summer of 1945, Grenier would introduce Guilloux to
Camus and they would become close friends.

Grenier's recommended reading proved to be a liberation
for the adolescent from Belcourt whose upbringing had left him
perplexed and hesitant. Years later, in 1948, Camus, by then a high-
profile writer, endorsed Guilloux's achievement in *The House of the
People* by providing a preface for a work which had so fired his
imagination.

He would likewise write an introduction to Grenier's *Les Iles*
(Islands) when it was republished in 1959. When that work first
appeared in 1933, it too mesmerized the young Camus. Made up of

a collection of essays, Grenier's work evokes the world of travel and reflects how certain places deliver the 'sight of a landscape [which] acts on us like a great musician playing on a very ordinary instrument'.[2] As Camus was to reflect in his Grenier preface, his teacher's work had served as a corrective, a quarter of a century earlier, to the world of sentient pleasure inhabited by the young Camus. He had grown up in poverty but life in Algiers also meant for him the pleasures of the beach and the body which, as he commented, cost nothing: 'we were living . . . in sensation, on the surface of the world, among colours, waves and the alluring smells of the earth.' Grenier's perspective spelled a different temperamental affinity, one that was revelatory, the mature Camus reflected in 1959: it 'initiated us to disenchantment; we had discovered culture'.[3] By which Camus meant that Grenier – not a Mediterranean but a Celt (he had gone to the same school in Saint-Brieuc as Louis Guilloux) – was announcing the impermanence of sentient pleasure.

As an avid young reader of Grenier in 1933, Camus drank all of this in. He went on to reflect modestly in his preface that this 'great theme from down the ages' had struck him as being intensely novel: 'We needed to be . . . pulled out of our happy barbarism.'[4] And the resulting state, Camus adds, was one in which doubt took hold, a productive doubt in that it was to feed into art. Camus evoked the image of the garden of art, one no less alluring, he commented, than the walled gardens up on the heights in Algiers whose invisible interiors – the homes of wealthy colonialists – were the subject of which he dreamt in his poverty.

Islands, then, served as a catalyst in 1933. In a conscious act of affiliation, Camus saw the essays as triggering in him the desire to write. It was a desire that was lived as a form of rebirth: 'Something, someone, was stirring in me, obscurely, and wanted to speak.'[5] By his own striking admission in his Grenier preface, Camus saw his earlier self as needing to learn submission and to accept the message of a spiritual master. Conscious of the tenor of the language he was using in 1959, he conceded that his was an unfashionable message in an age of 'half truths', when 'each consciousness pursues the death of the other' (he was referring in a pejorative way to the Hegelian notion then in vogue among left-wing intellectuals in France).[6]

In the autumn of 1932 Camus, in his late teens, began what was to be his final year at the lycée. He was entering 'hypokhâgne', part of a preparatory course of study designed to prepare students for the entrance examination to the Ecole Normale Supérieure. He was one of a dozen pupils in the class, male and female, and by then he cut a dapper figure. To his peers he seemed aloof, parading his highbrow tastes in reading.[7] With his fellow students largely middle-class, the young Camus was now part of a different social circle. When Jean Grenier moved with his family up to the Parc d'Hydra in the hills above the city in the summer of 1933, Camus was one of a group of talented young people who came to be invited regularly to the Greniers' home. After Camus' death in 1960, Grenier would look back on 30 years of 'mutual affection' and play down any sense of Camus' intellectual debt to him, choosing instead to quote from Dante: 'Poca favilla gran fiamma seconda' (from a small spark a great flame follows).[8]

Among Camus' contemporaries were the sculptor and painter Louis Bénisti, André Belamich who would go on to become a Hispanist, translating Lorca, and Max-Pol Fouchet, a future editor of the poetry review *Fontaine*. Also part of the group was Jean de Maisonseul, described by Fouchet as an aristocrat with a Proustian manner: he went on to be an architect and would later become curator of the renamed National Museum of Fine Art in post-independence Algeria.[9]

Fouchet's girlfriend, a glamorous young woman named Simone Hié, belonged to the same social set. The daughter of a middle-class family (her mother was an optometrist), she was to drop Fouchet and start a relationship with Camus. When he later announced to his uncle Gustave Acault his wish to marry Simone, Acault expressed his violent disapproval and Camus felt obliged to leave his uncle's home in 1933. After a spell living in the suburb of Hydra, in the summer he moved in with his older brother Lucien, who was living in the rue Michelet.[10] Simone Hié and Camus were married on 16 June 1934 and set up home in the Parc d'Hydra.

In the previous autumn, he had begun a two-year degree in philosophy at the University of Algiers and he followed this up with a postgraduate thesis (his DES) on Plotinus and Saint Augustine, completed in May 1936. His marriage to the attractive and talented Simone proved short-lived. She had a problem with drug addiction and the couple were to separate at the end of the summer of 1936 after a trip to central Europe during which Camus discovered that she was having an affair with the doctor who was prescribing her drugs. He described the sense of emptiness he felt during that fateful summer trip to central Europe in a short prose-text, 'La Mort dans l'âme' (Death in the Soul).

The text was evidence that Camus, who had been trying his hand at creative writing since his teens, was now moving forward on that front. But the progress came at a price. In a fictionalized autobiographical piece, the eponymous young hero Louis Raingeard anguishes about his relationship with his mother and reflects intensely on how his intellectual and aesthetic development risked excluding her: 'Each book discovered, each ever more refined emotional experience . . . pushed them further apart' (OC, I, 90–91).

The 'Louis Raingeard' material was to serve as a dry run for the collection L'Envers et l'endroit (The Wrong Side and the Right Side), a slim volume dedicated to Jean Grenier which was brought out in May 1937 by the young Algiers publisher Edmond Charlot, one of the circle of friends who used to gather at the Greniers' up in the Parc d'Hydra. The sense of the French title is of the right side of fabric (the *endroit*) as opposed to the side that is customarily not visible (the *envers*) and Camus used the metaphor to draw attention

A Moorish café in the Casbah, Algiers.

to what he saw as the regular blinkering of human perception: how the love of life goes hand in hand with, and yet often conceals, a despair at living.

The short texts that make up the collection lend themselves to a biographical reading. They draw on scenes of 1930s living marked by pessimism and an absence of glamour: in working-class Algiers, a generational divide spells the divorce between youthful male arrogance and the introspection and isolation of the elderly; a first-person narrator spends 'mortal days' in Prague (this is recounted in the 'Death in the Soul' text which was shaped by the break-up with Simone Hié in 1936); in a crowded café in Palma de Mallorca a woman dances sensuously, to the raucous approval of a male audience; and in a Moorish café in Algiers, an adult son recalls his mother sitting in silence as the life of the poor quarter filters through the window of the family apartment and he is struck by 'the indifference of that strange mother!' (*oc*, I, 50). In his mind's eye, Camus' protagonist evokes, alongside the sounds of the evening traffic and an accordion playing in the café below, the image of the withdrawn mother persisting with her knitting in spite of her arthritic hands (*oc*, I, 53).

The enigmatic figure of the mentally absent mother provides a centre of emotional gravity in Camus' early work. 'It begins with the voice of the woman who did not think' is how he introduces a previous draft of the same writing project entitled 'Les Voix du quartier pauvre' (Voices of the Poor Quarter), which he presented to his wife Simone Hié as a gift dated 25 December 1934.[11] Likewise, on the very first page of the *Carnets* or notebooks that Camus was to keep from May 1935 through to the end of his life, the complex mother–son link stands as something foundational: 'the bizarre feeling that the son has for his mother forms *his entire sensibility*'.[12]

Re-experiencing childhood is presented in *The Wrong Side and the Right Side* as a homecoming: 'And here I am repatriated. I think of a child who lived in a poor district. That district, that house!' (*oc*, I, 48). The biographical basis for the text is clear: the unlit stairwell at home, the child's instinctive horror of the cockroaches on the banisters, the stinking corridor, the chairs the family would bring downstairs and place at the front door of the building to enjoy the evening air at the end of the working day, and the compensation of nature: 'for those at the bottom of the social pile, the sky assumes its full meaning: it is a priceless grace' (*oc*, I, 49).

Camus' tableau is not only visual but psychological. There is nothing exuberant or celebratory about this return to the past. In particular the son's relationship to the mother is the subject of a tense, claustrophobic narrative. She cuts an acutely isolated figure, no more so than when she sits alone in the flat, with other family members yet to return home for the evening: 'Around her, as night falls, her mutism conveys an irremediable desolation' (*oc*, I, 49). For the young Camus, his mother's 'animal silence' marks not only her distance but his emotional confusion, unable as he is to work out if his pity for her amounts to love.

That Camus, often reticent about revealing private emotion, came to channel this raw feeling into literature was due in no small measure to the intervention of Jean Grenier. When André Gide died in 1951, Camus provided a text for inclusion in a collective tribute put together by the Gallimard publishing house to honour its distinguished employee (Camus himself also worked there from late 1943 onwards). In Camus' eulogy, he recalled his first contact with the work of the deceased author, who was more than 40 years his senior. It was Gustave Acault who had introduced his nephew to Gide's tribute to the life of the senses, *Les Nourritures Terrestres* (The Fruits of the Earth). But no less eye-catching in Camus' tribute to the canonical figure of Gide is his miraculous reading encounter with the minor writer André de Richaud. Camus describes how, just as his uncle had 'held out a book' – a copy of the Gide – so Jean Grenier had steered him towards *Grief*.

Richaud's book was, Camus explained to his reader, the first one 'to speak to me about what I knew' (*oc*, III, 881), namely the world of poverty, a mother who was a war widow and the beauty of evenings reflected in the sky. Camus went on to suggest the deeply therapeutic character of literature: *Grief* 'untied, deep within me, a knot of obscure links and delivered me from shackles the embarrassment of which I felt without being able to name them' (*oc*, III, 882). Having read the book through in a night, he describes himself as experiencing a new freedom in relation to what was sayable: 'I took my first hesitant steps on an unknown land.' Reading Richaud was thus an emancipation. That said, the expressive range in *The Wrong Side and the Right Side* was to remain inhibited: Camus evokes the complex bond between mother and son and yet important elements of that link remain understated in the catch-all formulation, *la part obscure* (the obscure side of emotions). In what was to be his last interview, given on 20 December 1959, Camus spoke of 'what is blind and instinctive in me', a side of his work which literary criticism in France, being interested primarily in ideas, he believed, had overlooked (*oc*, IV, 661). Richaud's *Grief* makes explicit a mother's oppressive attachment to her son in the absence of the father killed in the First World War. Indeed in Richaud, the misdirection of emotional intensity comes close to sexualizing the maternal feeling. By contrast, Camus' portrait of the mother is characterized by her frequent emotional absence.

In a letter of 8 July 1937 to his friend Jean de Maisonseul, who had been encouraging in his response to the short volume *The Wrong Side and the Right Side* published by Charlot, Camus insisted that the book was not a work of the intelligence. It was, he suggested, his heart and his flesh that had written it (*oc*, I, 97). This emotional and bodily connection to the writing would be reaffirmed twenty years later when Camus argued in a preface for the 1958 republication of the work (this time with Gallimard) that 'there is more true love in these awkward pages than in all those that have followed' (*oc*, I, 31–2). He made much of the power of what is 'muted and unformulated' (*oc*, IV, 1285), as we saw in the Introduction. In a diary entry of 1937, he reflected that if he had to write a book on morality, it would contain 100 pages, 99 of which would be blank 'and on the last page I would write: "I know only one duty and that is to love."'[13]

3

'This Algiers Happiness'

Camus' school friend Max-Pol Fouchet was no reactionary colonialist and indeed he would go on to oppose French Army oppression at the height of the Algerian War in the late 1950s. He nevertheless conceded in a 1968 memoir in relation to the French Algerian experience that

> there was an Algerian and an Algiers happiness, there is no point in denying that. I don't believe I am suspect, people know what I wanted for Algeria, but I recognize that this Algiers happiness is part of our memory and something we hold dear. We were happy, even we poor adolescents, while being conscious of the misery of others, the injustice meted out to Muslims.

Fouchet added that French Algerians guarded their happiness 'blindly, ferociously, fiercely sometimes'.[1]

The idea of colonial Algiers as a playground also held meaning for French metropolitan bourgeois writers such as Gide, author of *The Fruits of the Earth* as we have seen and, a generation later, Henry de Montherlant. Montherlant wrote in cavalier terms of his time spent there in the late 1920s: 'My love for Algiers has spared the public half a dozen books which I have not written because the city invited me to enjoy life instead of scribbling away on paper.'[2] But if the outsider Montherlant saw Algiers as a distraction from the business of literary composition, growing up in Algiers was an experience that Camus was keen to commit to paper.

In the essay 'L'Eté à Alger' (Summer in Algiers) he provides a brief sketch of life in the colonial city. At the same time the text offers elements of an individual self-portrait to the extent that many of the attitudes of the city's European settler population were, unsurprisingly, Camus' own. The essay was one of four pieces written in 1936–7 and grouped together under the title *Noces* (Nuptials). As had been the case with *The Wrong Side and the Right Side*, it was the Algiers publisher Edmond Charlot, by then still only 24, who brought out the work in May 1939.

'Summer in Algiers' conveys the lifestyle not of metropolitan bourgeois *flâneurs* like Montherlant but of the city's working-class European settler inhabitants. These were the people Camus came from and he provided an insider's understanding of their mentality. He charted their speech habits and noted the directness of their

3Boulevard de la République, Boulevard Anatole France and the Consular Palace on the Algiers seafront.

manner, which could quickly tip over into aggressiveness.
The essay includes a street scene in which young men involved in
a brawl recount their exploits in the local *Cagayous* dialect.
The ironic vignette allows its author to record the bragging and
machismo that were part of French Algerian culture. Yet behind
the bravado he detects vulnerability. In the working-class districts
of Belcourt and Bab-el-Oued, people marry young, he observes,
and for a worker of 30, his best days are already behind him.

Camus writes perceptively of lives being consumed in an
intense, unexamined way. In colonial Algiers religious notions of
virtue and hell hold no sway with European settlers who have a
natural affinity with the rogue, he comments. The rudiments of a
'code of the street' (*oc*, I, 122), a male-authored code, prevail: looking after one's mother, ensuring respect for one's wife, displaying
concern for pregnant women and fighting clean in the street – that
is to say, *mano-a-mano* with one's adversary.

Camus' depiction of 1930s Algiers was oddly both admiring and
unflattering. Its inhabitants enjoy the sky and the easy access to the
sea, he argues, but city life offers little in the way of intellectual
stimulation: 'There is nothing here for those wanting to learn, to
educate themselves and to become better' (*oc*, I, 117). The city's
young men – and again Camus' focus is on the European population – may enjoy the pleasure of being on the beach, looking out
over the bay and flirting with young women. But once youth has
passed, the city holds no consolation. Europe may have its church
architecture and attractive landscapes to mask the inevitability of
ageing, Camus suggests, but Algiers offers no such aesthetic
redemption. Old men sit impassively in the working-class bars of
Belcourt and Bab-el-Oued while young males brag.

With its often acerbic tone, 'Summer in Algiers' provides early
evidence of Camus' appetite for trenchant characterization. He dis-
misses the claims of professional thinkers with their theories about
the freedom of the flesh. In a place like Algiers, he insists, cerebral

reflection on the subject of bodily pleasure is every bit as irrelevant as Christianity's mistrust of the flesh. That Camus recognizes the young European men around him as his 'brothers' (*oc*, I, 120) confirms the element of self-portrait in the essay. He cites admiringly the uncomplicated hedonism of a male friend who works in a factory, is a junior swimming champion and chases after pretty young women. In the city's cinemas, mint pastilles bearing love messages are exchanged by couples, this often serving as a basis for entry into marriage in districts like Belcourt. 'And this', Camus asserts, 'accurately depicts the infant people of this country' (*oc*, I, 121). In the dance hall on the Padovani beach, youths from the poor quarter dance away the hours.

In these impressions of everyday life in the Algiers of the 1930s, Camus' focus was squarely on the city's European population. Indeed he was conscious that his narrative of pleasure-seeking was an ethnocentric one. In the Place du Gouvernement, native Algerians selling glasses of chilled lemon squash play an ancillary role while in the Moorish cafés of the Casbah, 'the body is silent' as clients drink tea (*oc*, I, 120). Camus himself thus relativizes and situates the parade of hedonism in 'Summer in Algiers'.

That not everything fell under the 'Algiers happiness' rubric signalled by Max-Pol Fouchet is also in evidence when Camus evokes the lives of the over-thirties within the city's working-class European population. They play bowls, go to the cinema and form friendly associations. As he writes almost matter-of-factly, 'without religion and without idols, they die alone at the end of lives lived collectively' (*oc*, I, 122). Camus is scathing about the Christian cemetery on the Boulevard Bru, deriding the lavish promises of eternal memory made to the dead and the tacky emblems that adorn the burial places (flower bouquets made of stucco, a toy aeroplane incongruously piloted by a winged angel and so on). And yet a residual loyalty persists in his evocation of the European Algerians. They can be unjust, he concedes. But he wonders – in

An Algiers street scene of the interwar years: 'La Saucisse à Michel'
(Michel's Sausages).

what he admits is an 'insane hope' (*oc*, I, 124) – if the ability of
the residents of Belcourt and Bab-el-Oued to live in the present,
without the consolations of myth, literature and religion, might
not have the makings of a redemptive philosophical outlook. In
Camus' formulation, in their refusal to hope in an eternal destiny,

'La Villa des Fresques' (The Villa of the Frescoes) at the ancient Roman ruins of Tipasa in Algeria.

they avoid sinning against life (*oc*, I, 125). The *Nuptials* narrative thus not only constructs a collective mindset but signals important elements in Camus' individual psychology and outlook.

Reminding his reader that for the ancient Greeks one of the ills that came out of Pandora's box was the human reliance on hope, Camus approves the settlers' lucid, obdurate acceptance of life in its impermanence. In 'Le Vent à Djémila' (The Wind at Djémila), also in the *Nuptials* collection, he is forthright: 'the belief that death opens on to another life is something I find disagreeable' (*oc*, I, 113). The same impatience with any idea of an afterlife is to be found in his projected autobiographical novel *Louis Raingeard* which he had been working on in the years 1934–6: its third chapter was to have carried the title 'Our Kingdom is of This World'.[3]

For the author of *Nuptials*, then, the very ordinary lives of settlers bring both disappointment and inspiration. As someone whose own trajectory was taking him towards writing, Camus was struck by their anti-intellectualism: 'This race is indifferent to the things of the mind. It has the cult . . . of the body' (*oc*, I, 123). Yet he holds on to the hope that they might be the improbable bearers of a stoic message about human mortality.

In the summer of 1935 Camus had embarked on a cargo ship heading for Tunisia but a recurrence of illness forced him to abandon the trip. Back in Algiers, he recovered and was able in late August to visit Tipasa, situated on the Algerian coast at the foot of the Chenoua mountain. It was a site of Roman ruins and before that had been a Phoenician trading post. 'Noces à Tipasa' (Nuptials at Tipasa), the opening essay in the collection, describes how, for the young writer, immersion in the world of ancient stone brought an immediacy of connection at a sensory level. Camus found hypnotic the aromatic profusion generated by the hibiscus, iris, bougainvillea and broom. In the ruins themselves, the smell of wormwood, he wrote, was everywhere. Emphasizing sensuous enjoyment, he described the quasi-erotic pleasure of the human body, covered in the perfume of plants and plunging into the sea. He chided those who would spurn this hedonism: 'There is no shame in being happy . . . to my mind the person who is afraid to enjoy is a fool' (*oc*, I, 108). All the while, the sentience and self-absorption of the scene is unapologetic. Camus was not alone in recording his solipsistic pleasure-seeking. In September 1948 Simone de Beauvoir would also visit Tipasa, describing the experience as a rejuvenating contact with nature: 'breathing in an ancient smell of sun and scrub . . . suddenly I was twenty again: neither regrets nor expectation, just the earth and the water and my life'.[4]

Travel to Tuscany in late summer 1937 provided Camus with another lesson in acceptance of the present. In the final essay in *Nuptials*, 'Le Désert' (The Desert), he enthused about Piero della Francesca's depiction of the risen Christ. In the subject's face, Camus saw not otherworldliness but rather a greatness or *grandeur* which he interprets as a will to live, 'for the sage like the idiot expresses little' (*oc*, I, 136). During the same trip to Italy, he visited a Franciscan monastery in Fiesole. There, too, he was keen not to depict sanctity as looking beyond this world. Camus was energized by the thought that the monks practised an ascetic lifestyle in order to have access to a fuller life in the here and now and he links this back to the youths from settler families on the Padovani beach in Algiers. In his view, what linked the monks and the pleasure-seekers was that they were all in love with life. Of the religious community in Florence, he writes that 'if they divest themselves of possessions, it's in order to live a greater life (and not aspire to another life)' (*oc*, I, 133).

Camus could see the provocation in his pairing of asceticism and hedonism and yet the connection allowed him to conclude that the world around him was itself an invitation to live life fully. (Later, the artist figure Jonas would arrive at a similar conclusion in the short story bearing his name in the 1957 collection *L'Exil et le Royaume* (Exile and the Kingdom)). Giotto's portraits of St Francis convey what Camus refers to as the 'inner smile' that serves to 'justify those who have the taste for happiness' (*oc*, I, 133). In a notebook entry for the same month (September 1937), he recorded his enthusiasm for 'Francis [of Assisi], lover of nature and of life' (*oc*, II, 829). Camus was thus busy in *Nuptials* giving expression to an intense commitment to living in the present. His experience of tuberculosis and sense of life's fragility had given urgency and energy to that perspective.

Writing in Oran in 1939, in a piece entitled 'Le Minotaure ou la halte d'Oran' (The Minotaur or The Stop at Oran),[5] Camus reflected on the rivalry between that coastal city, situated on the western side of Algeria, and Algiers. As with his depiction of the colonial capital, Camus chose a scene of working-class masculinity in Oran as his point of access to local culture, with a thousand men crowding into a makeshift boxing arena for an evening's entertainment. The result of the main contest between an Oranese fighter and his opponent, a French Navy champion, was a draw – frustrating for a crowd used to having a winner and a loser. In Camus' mocking formulation, their 'Manichean sensibility' is affronted by this insipid outcome, though when both fighters embrace at the end of the contest, the crowd roars its approval. Still, if male bonding lay at the heart of the European Algerian world that Camus was describing, he could be ironic as well as solemn in his evocation, as when he describes how, with fighting breaking out among the spectators themselves, the organizers rushed to restore order by playing a rousing military march, 'Sambre et Meuse', on the record player. It was half as an insider, half as an ethnographer that Camus was evoking European settler life. In 'The Minotaur', physical violence, male touchiness and a splash of military fervour are all part and parcel of the collective imaginary of the European Algerian.

Camus was thus intensely alive to the anti-intellectual milieu of colonial Algeria. In *The Plague*, he would describe the inhabitants of Oran as having 'simple passions' (*oc*, ii, 81), a variant on the 'infant people' (*oc*, i, 121) label which he used in 'Summer in Algiers'. As a writer, he was also conscious of the shift from the immediacy of experience to the process of mediation that came with textual composition: 'There is a time for living and a time for bearing witness to living. There is . . . a time to create, which is less natural' (*oc*, i, 109), he reflected. In later years, Camus would wrestle with the shift to the 'less natural', complaining about the isolation which the business of writing entailed.

In a 1947 essay with the striking title 'Petit guide pour des villes sans passé' (A Short Guide for Towns without a Past), Camus contrasted Algeria and Europe. In the process, he relied on the clichéd colonial view that before the arrival of the European there was somehow nothing. Algerian towns offered no aesthetic stimulation, he suggested, unlike Toledo for example, with its El Greco heritage, and many of the Italian cities. In a bantering tone, he seeks to dissuade 'the very delicate minds, the aesthetes and the newly-weds' (*oc*, III, 593) from visiting Algeria. When Parisians say they want to come, he playfully discourages them and points to what separates the two cultures: French Algerians will be your friends but, being extrovert, they are not given to confiding in people whereas for Parisians the flow of confidences is endless in what Camus describes, tongue-in-cheek, as a 'great spending of the soul' (*oc*, III, 594). By contrast, he claims to find compensation in the beauty and appeal of Algeria's young people: the country's Arabs, in his formulation, and its settler community – 'a bastard race' with Jews, Greeks, Spanish, and people from Alsace and Italy and Malta all thrown together.[6]

What emerges from Camus' writing of the 1930s therefore is a certain idea of Algeria. The conflictual history of French colonial relations there would intensify his sense of connection while making it an increasingly more anxious one. He drew on mythology to underline that allegiance. Writing in 'L'Exil d'Hélène' (The Exile of Helen, 1948), he observed that when Ulysses was offered the choice between immortality and his fatherland, he opted for the latter and with it mortality (*oc*, III, 600). But choosing Algeria could by his own admission skew Camus' perspective. He argued that having been born in 'this desert', he could not speak of it as a visitor: 'I thus have with Algeria a long relationship that will no doubt never finish and which prevents me from being altogether clear-sighted in relation to it' (*oc*, III, 594).

4

All Work and No Play

Given Camus' working-class colonial background, the progression
to his being a public figure and best-selling author was far from
automatic. Long before he managed to establish himself as a professional writer, he had turned his hand to various things. He grew up
in a milieu dominated, as we have seen, by the culture of manual
labour. Whereas the middle-class districts of Algiers saw an exodus
during the hot summers as the well-to-do and the colonial bureau-
crats went off on vacation to 'recuperate in the good "French air"'
(*FM*, 200), neighbourhoods like Belcourt saw no such movement.
    Life there was dominated by work. Camus recalls in *The First
Man* how the absence of paid holidays for employees (this would
change with the election of the Popular Front in France in 1936)
made members of Jacques' family hostile towards workers of different ethnic backgrounds – they would complain about Jews, Arabs,
Italians and Spaniards taking their work. Camus was writing much
of *The First Man* in 1959, by which stage his public opposition to
Communism was long established. He was thus being provocative
in drawing attention to the family attitude of hostility, insisting
that, however much it went against Marxist theories of proletarian
struggle, the resentment against workers from different ethnicities
had to be understood against the background of economic insecurity
that gave rise to it (*FM*, 200).
    Money was scarce at home in Belcourt and as a secondary-
school teenager Camus was obliged to find work during the

summer holidays. *The First Man* charts the adolescent's initiation to the world of paid employment. His maternal grandmother, Catherine Sintès, born in the middle of the nineteenth century, had never been to school. Having worked as a child herself, she could not see why, for a period of three months each year, her schoolboy grandson should remain idle. There was little chance of him getting a temporary job, however, and so when he was thirteen, they went to a hardware store in the Agha district of the city near the port. There the grandmother claimed that her grandson was having to give up the lycée because of a lack of money at home and on that basis he was taken on, earning 150 francs a month for an eight-hour day. (Years later, the job came, improbably, to make the headlines when, with fame beckoning in the wake of the success of Camus' novel *The Plague*, an Italian newspaper headline read 'Before *The Plague*, he was selling bolts').[1] As that summer came to an end and with school beckoning, the truth of the boy's situation had to be revealed, to the moral outrage of the employer and the shame of a tearful young Camus. In a deeply conflicted recollection of that humiliation, he would go on to write:

> To lie for the right to have no holiday, to work far from the summer sky and the sea he so loved, and to lie again for the right to return to his work at the *lycée* – this injustice made him desperately unhappy (*FM*, 213).

At the same time, the strain to make ends meet at home explained the emotion felt by the adolescent now able to contribute to the family budget.

Camus viscerally resented the numbing impact of much organized labour. He recalled in *The First Man* how the sight of people regularly commuting at the end of a long day showed him that work was hard and life short. Prior to that, 'he had only known the riches and the joys of poverty' (*FM*, 210). These lessons helped shape the libertarian perspective that was to become his hallmark. The summers of his youth spent working for employers who believed he was there on a permanent basis came to be viewed as 'summers sacrificed to the misery of the lie' (*FM*, 213). Later, in the 1950s, with his work attracting political controversy, the act of writing would itself become alienating labour for a disillusioned Camus.

Yet two forms of work come to be differentiated in a revealing reflection contained in a short journalistic piece which appeared in *L'Express* in May 1955. While noting the male-centred language of his day, we find Camus singing the praises of creative collective endeavour:

> I have never been happy, I know, nor pacified, except in a craft [*métier*] worthy of faith, in work taken forward with men I can love. I know too that in this regard many people are like me. Without work, life rots away. But under the weight of a soulless toil, life becomes stifled and withers (*oc*, III, 1016).

For the adolescent Camus, the routine of office work, with all the detailed record-keeping associated with buying and selling, was nothing more than 'vulgarity'. He could only contrast that with the world of the small factory where his Uncle Etienne worked and which he visited as a boy. There, the coopers turned out barrels for use in the wine industry. As he records in *The First Man*, the work required 'a lengthy physical effort, a series of skilful, precise actions by hard, quick-moving hands – and you saw the result of your labour take shape: a new barrel, well finished . . . something the worker could contemplate' (*FM*, 208). Camus was alert to the appeal of manual dexterity and *homo faber*, man as a maker of artefacts, was a source of celebration for him.

One of his summer jobs as an adolescent involved working in the offices of an Algiers shipbroker, again on the pretence ('the misery of the lie') that he had left school. It was a job which Camus the writer would pass on to Meursault in *The Outsider*. Relief from office boredom came in the form of errands within the city, for example to the main post office.

Life in the shipbroker's office also brought new experiences, if we accept the account provided by *The First Man*. When Jacques Cormery inadvertently sees between the legs of a female office worker, a mystery is aroused in him, the narrator tells his reader, which the many erotic encounters of his adult life would never subsequently dispel (*FM*, 209).

Working for the shipbroker, whose premises looked out on to the Boulevard Front-de-mer, also meant visits to the ships docked close by. The early decades of the twentieth century had seen the port in Algiers significantly developed and indeed in what in the days of empire was known as 'la plus grande France', or 'the greater France', it was to become one of the nation's principal ports. The young Camus was born into this world of colonial mercantile

The Hôtel des Postes, Algiers. This monument to colonial exuberance and ambition was described by Camus in *The First Man*: 'The post office itself, in an immense rotunda, was lit by three large doors and light trickling through a large cupola' (*FM*, 208).

The interior of the Hôtel des Postes, Algiers.

The busy port of Algiers, which the young Camus would have known from his days at secondary school, having worked there as a clerk for a shipping agent one summer.

expansion. As a shipbroker's clerk, he enjoyed the vastness of the quays, going on board foreign vessels and translating documents for customs purposes. He could see close-up the hard physical labour of the dockers, stripped to the waist with sacks draped over their heads as they carried ashore bags of cement and coal, shuttling quickly between the quay and the boat in heat that made the tarmac melt. The sensualist and the dreamer in him noted the fragrance of the wood in ships arriving from Norway, the aroma of coffee from Dakar and Brazil, and the smell of wine (Camus' father's trade) as coastal vessels transporting cargo along the Algerian shoreline came into port.

Like his fictional counterpart Jacques Cormery, the teenage Camus was drawn to the cramped accommodation of sailors on board ship, preferring their living quarters to images of bourgeois luxury. He was also intrigued by the strange looks on the sailors' faces, looks that reflected their solitary lives (little wonder that he was an avid reader of Melville's *Moby Dick*). But by the end of the summer, thinner and exhausted after weeks on end working in the heat of the port, the schoolboy was ready to resume his twelve-hour days at the lycée.

These spells of temporary work sharpened Camus' view of conventional employment and the social conformism that went with it. In his early twenties, he would go on to try his hand at

The arcade of the Préfecture looking out onto the seafront in Algiers.

numerous things, working as a part-time tutor, for example, in 1934, and that summer in the driving licence office, which was located in the Préfecture of Algiers. Whether working in an iron-monger's or handling shipbroker's papers or doing other run-of-the-mill clerical work, Camus was all the while absorbing the material culture of his day in colonial Algiers. Frequently in his fiction we find protagonists engaged in the humdrum world of everyday work. Meursault knows office boredom in *The Outsider* and on his lunch break enjoys the physical release of running to hop a lift on a lorry as it passes noisily along the quayside (*oc*, I, 155); the mundane keeping of records comes to be thrown into relief in the state of emergency that is declared in *The Plague*; and in 'The Silent Ones' in *Exile and the Kingdom*, hard manual labour leaves the alienated factory workers who give the story its title physically spent. In the philosophical essay *Le Mythe de Sisyphe* (The Myth of Sisyphus), which would appear in 1942, Camus draws out the drama in the divine punishment imposed on Sisyphus, who must repeatedly roll his rock to the top of the mountain. Tellingly, however, Camus prefers to think of his hero in the interludes between intense physical toil as he comes back down the mountain and savours the moments of lucidity and reflectiveness: 'Sisyphus, a proletarian who is subject to the gods, impotent and in revolt, knows the full extent of his miserable condition. On this his thoughts are focussed during his descent' (*oc*, I, 302–3).

5

A Beautiful Profession

My body demands [I write].

Camus' protagonist Patrice Mersault, *A Happy Death* (*oc*, ii, 811)

The lesson of lives consumed by physical effort, to say nothing of
Camus' own experience of illness, gave drive and urgency to what
he did and he was active both politically and culturally in the
1930s. Encouraged by Jean Grenier and Claude de Fréminville, he
joined the Parti Communiste Algérien (Algerian Communist Party)
in 1935. In 1936 he represented the Party in the anti-Fascist
Amsterdam-Pleyel Movement where Max-Pol Fouchet was a young
socialist delegate. But having complained about Communist hostility towards Messali Hadj's Algerian nationalist group, L'Etoile
Nord-Africaine (The North African Star), he was accused of being a
Trotskyite and was soon to resign.[1]

Camus was versatile and had drive, and on joining the
Algerian Communist Party, he had thrown himself into local
cultural initiatives in Algiers, helping to set up an amateur dramatic group, the Théâtre du Travail (Theatre of Work) in the
autumn of 1935 and a Maison de la Culture (House of Culture).
In November 1936 he secured some theatre work with Radio-Alger.
As he was to explain more than twenty years later in an interview
for *Paris-Théâtre*, Algiers had been a desert back then as far as
theatre was concerned (*oc*, iv, 577). With his friends Yves
Bourgeois, Alfred Poignant and Jeanne-Paule Sicard at the Théâtre

Trotskyism: branch of marxism
Leon Trotsky, Russian - Ukranian
- anti stalin & S.U.

du Travail, he co-authored *Révolte dans les Asturies* (Revolt in Asturias). The play depicted the struggle of mineworkers in northwest Spain against an oppressive political regime in 1934. But in a politically motivated move, the right-wing mayor of Algiers, Augustin Rozis, denied the players access to a theatre in April 1936, meaning that the play was not performed although the publisher Edmond Charlot brought out a small print-run of the work. The group did however succeed in putting on adaptations of works by writers such as Malraux, Gorky, Aeschylus, Pushkin and Ben Jonson. In October 1937 the group morphed into the Théâtre de l'Equipe (The Team Theatre), which put on an adaptation of Dostoyevsky's *The Brothers Karamazov* in May of the following year, with Camus in the role of Ivan.

Camus remained intensely conscious of what for him was the almost visceral pull of writing. In 1936, in some preparatory notes for *La Mort heureuse* (A Happy Death), he attributes to the character Patrice Mersault the thought that 'I have to write just as I have to swim, since my body demands it' (*oc*, II, 811). In September 1937 Camus turned down a teaching job in Sidi-bel-Abbès in the department of Oran, giving as the reason his fear that the work would involve too much routine. Instead he took up a temporary post at the Algiers Institute of Meteorology, working there from November 1937 until the following September.[2] In 1939 he declined another school post, this time as a Latin teacher in the Bouzareah Lycée on the outskirts of Algiers.

All the while, Camus was pressing ahead with his literary projects. In his notebook in August 1937, in an early mention of what was to mutate into *The Outsider*, he referred to a character who, having tried to live conventionally through marriage and getting a job, came to realize that life as described in the fashion catalogue he was reading was not for him (*oc*, II, 824). The year 1938 saw him finish *Nuptials* and undertake preparatory work both for *Caligula* and *The Outsider*.

Journalism, 'one of the most beautiful professions I know', as he was later to remark, was another forum that allowed Camus to pursue his desire to write.[3] It had the additional attraction of drawing him into the community formed by those composing and materially producing the printed word. Like the world of the theatre, working on a newspaper gave him a feeling of collective involvement and he thrived on the energy that came from this shared enterprise.

The way into journalism was facilitated by Pascal Pia, who had been recruited in France to be editor-in-chief of a new Algiers paper that would be sympathetic to the left-wing Front Populaire, which had come to power in France in the elections back in May 1936. *Alger républicain* was a paper with a modest circulation, financed by its left-wing European Algerian shareholders, many of them public servants and artisans opposed to the rise of Fascism. It was launched on 6 October 1938. A year later, with the outbreak of war and paper in short supply, Pia decided to switch to a two-page format but the renamed *Le Soir Républicain* quickly fell victim to the wartime censors. The paper was shut down by the Government General of Algeria in January 1940.

Back in October 1938, the first issue of *Alger républicain* set out its aims. It would seek to provide genuinely democratic coverage of the life of the city. 'From Belcourt to Bab-el-Oued', wrote one of its journalists, Lucienne Jean-Darrouy, 'we will listen to people and events with equal attention; we will explore the humblest street and the most sordid quarters of the city in an attempt to understand the source of their shame or their distress . . . We will explore everyday life and reflect on what the country owes its inhabitants, whether they be Muslim or Christian.'[4]

Needing to keep the wage bill low, Pascal Pia was looking to recruit young, inexpensive talent. He took on Camus as an editor and also gave him the run of a literary section, *Le Salon de lecture* (The Reading Room). In the latter role, Camus could pursue his keen interest in contemporary literature and among the works he reviewed were Sartre's *La Nausée* (Nausea, 20 October 1938), Henry de Montherlant's *L'Equinoxe de septembre* (September Equinox, 5 February 1939) and a work by Ignazio Silone in French translation, *Le Pain et le Vin* (Bread and Wine, 23 May 1939). On 14 September 1939 Camus began serialization of Louis Guilloux's *La Maison du peuple*, one of the novels Jean Grenier had urged him to read back at the lycée. But a book containing talk of workers' solidarity and with a rendition of the Socialist 'Internationale' as part of its storyline was not long in attracting the attention of the censors, who blocked the novel's publication five days later, prompting staff on the paper to leave a large blank space on the page with the message that serialization would resume shortly.

For Camus, one of the lessons learnt from reading Guilloux's novel was that, in the words of its cobbler protagonist who campaigns for social justice, 'people cannot stem the flow of ideas.'[5] Certainly there was no shortage of campaigning energy in Camus' work for *Alger républicain*. He was a novice in the field, as were many of his colleagues. But he was not afraid to take on the power of vested interests and he quickly found his feet, adopting an often strongly moral tone. He criticized the mayor of Algiers, Augustin Rozis, for failing to protect its citizens when a gas explosion claimed lives in rue Blanchard.

Camus was no less tenacious in his reporting of court work and fought successfully to defend a state employee, Michel Hodent, who had been wrongly accused of profiteering in the handling of stocks of wheat produced by native Algerian farmers. In a style of journalism reminiscent of Zola's 'J'accuse' at the time of the Dreyfus Affair, Camus sent an open letter to the Governor General on 10 January 1939 protesting against the injustice of Hodent's imprisonment. The campaign succeeded. Years later, on news of Camus' sudden death in January 1960, Hodent would write from Ouargla in the Sahara to Camus' widow, Francine, to convey his continuing sense of indebtedness: 'I owe everything to him who is no more . . . nothing is forgotten.'[6] The Hodent Affair had shown the power of wealthy colonial landowners who were out to expropriate the land of indigenous farmers. But Camus was already well aware of the hold of reactionary politics in colonial Algeria in the 1930s, having seen the staging of the co-authored *Revolt in Asturias* obstructed by the mayor back in 1936.

The copy he produced for *Alger républicain* provided early evidence of what he was to later call his 'almost organic intolerance' (*oc*, III, 454) of injustice.[7] On 1 December 1938 he reported on a large prison ship, *Le Martinière*, that was anchored in the port of Algiers. Camus went on board and spoke briefly to a guard before becoming aware of a sound coming from the hold, 'like an inhuman breathing. That's where the *relégués* [the socially relegated] are' (*oc*, I, 586), he observed. With a fresh group of convicts being taken on board in Algiers for deportation to a penal colony, Camus invited readers to reflect on the inhuman 'relegation' whereby 'men are erased from humanity'. Empathizing with the plight of the newly embarked life prisoners, he protested: 'Today, they come down to the edge of this land which is theirs, to a few feet from the water' (*oc*, I, 587). Of those already held in the prison cages located in the hold of the vessel, the young journalist confessed to having difficulty seeing any resemblance between them and the world in which he was living. Camus concluded that his emotion was not one of pity: 'There is no more abject spectacle than to see people who have been reduced to a level beneath that of the human condition' (*oc*, I, 588). This campaigning journalism reflected Camus' attitude to the penal culture of his day and was to anticipate his vigorous opposition to the death penalty in the years after the Second World War.

Given the atmosphere of bitter recrimination that would later accompany France's loss of empire in Algeria and the scrutiny to which Camus' role as a public figure there was to be subjected, his reporting in 1939 on the socio-economic conditions obtaining in Kabylia in the eastern part of the country merits close attention. His 'Misère de la Kabylie' (Destitution in Kabylia) was the result of a trip made to the region that year at a time of famine. Stories of famine affecting the indigenous population were frequent in 1930s Algeria although the Algiers press was not a forum for such news.[8] In 1937 Camus' mentor Jean Grenier had himself written about the prevalence of hunger among native Algerians for the *Nouvelle Revue française*, but the conspicuous brevity of the piece with its reduced font size – Grenier was constructing an imagined dialogue between a self-satisfied colonialist and a more sceptical European voice – reflected the low level of interest among metropolitan readers of the day in the affairs of Algeria.[9] Between 5 and 15 June 1939, Camus published eleven articles in *Alger républicain*, seven of which were later to feature in the volume that drew together his writings on Algeria over a twenty-year period between 1939 and 1958, *Actuelles III. Chroniques algériennes* (Algerian Chronicles).[10]

Camus reported on the malnutrition affecting schoolchildren and on a general state of extreme poverty in Kabylia. In the *douar* or tribal village of Beni-Sliem, 96 per cent of the population, he wrote, were living in destitution (*oc*, IV, 313). He cited a case of food aid being denied in the Issers area to those who had supported Messali Hadj's moderate Algerian nationalist party, the PPA or Parti Populaire Algérien (Popular Algerian Party, *oc*, IV, 314). Camus went further, insisting that a system of slavery obtained in Kabylia (*oc*, IV, 316). He expressed moral outrage about a situation in which those recruited to work programmes designed to help them stave off hunger were forced to pay tax arrears, leaving them trapped in destitution. Such a practice amounted to 'an intolerable exploitation of human suffering' (*oc*, IV, 315). In documenting the extent of the poverty of the region, he argued that instead of charity, a solution built on 'a constructive social politics' (*oc*, IV, 314) was required.

Camus voiced his contempt for the paternalism of politicians such as Albert Lebrun, then president of the Third French Republic, who played down the gravity of the situation by stressing the great Kabyle capacity for resourcefulness and sobriety. The truth, Camus countered, was that in economic terms the Kabyles were three centuries behind European Algerians. He referred to his survey of the slave wages that were paid as 'that revolting enumeration' (*oc*, IV, 318) and he wrote of 'an abject logic' (*oc*, IV, 319) which saw starving workers paid less because of their reduced physical ability. In the same vein he asked why, at a time of pressing need for food, the main concern of the colonial authorities seemed to be awarding military medals to Algerians who had fought for France in the First World War.

By any standards, Camus' reporting on living conditions in Kabylia in the summer of 1939 conveyed a resolute engagement with the plight of the victims of colonial rule. He extended his intervention to the fields of education and economic and political development before concluding with reflections on what his role was. Anticipating the likely reception his reporting would trigger in colonialist circles, he stressed that to call for reform was not to be disloyal to France. Predictably, the right-wing paper *La Dépêche algérienne* dismissed his reporting and instead vaunted the colonial achievements of the French in Kabylia.

At the time of Camus' 'Destitution in Kabylia' work, French rule in the country appeared hegemonic, in spite of the fact that the 1930s had seen Muslim unrest. The March 1937 constitution of Messali Hadj's PPA had called for 'neither assimilation nor separation but emancipation'. On 14 July that year, the PPA had demonstrated in the streets of Algiers, demanding land reform, an Algerian parliament and respect for Islam.[11] Camus never contested the principle of the French presence in Algeria but he was calling for significant economic and political reform. On joining the Communist Party, he had been given the

his role in the communist party

role of developing relations with the country's indigenous populations. He was not particularly well equipped to do this, having little
knowledge of native cultures and speaking neither Berber nor the
local variant of Arabic, but when the Algerian Communist Party
dropped its opposition to colonialist politics, he resigned in protest
in September 1937. Earlier that year, the Popular Front government
in France had attempted to introduce modest reform in Algeria, the
so-called Blum-Viollette proposals (the plan being to enfranchise a
small native Algerian elite of about 20,000; at that time the total
Muslim population in the country numbered over six million).
Camus had actively supported the Blum-Viollette initiative, which
was not surprisingly opposed by Messali Hadj and other Algerian
nationalists who saw the measure as having a divisive impact on
Muslim Algeria. As for the country's European population, the great
majority was hostile to any reform and when the bill was due to be
put to a final vote in Paris in March 1938, 320 Algerian mayors
resigned in protest, prompting the proposals to be withdrawn.[12]

If the social deprivation described in 'Destitution in Kabylia' did
not represent an exceptional state of affairs in colonial Algeria but
rather was symptomatic of the wider policy of colonial expropriation in rural Algeria, Camus' intervention needs to be read against
the continuing backdrop of reactionary colonialist politics.[13]
In presentational terms, his trenchant reporting included much in
the way of facts and statistics but also some rhetorical flourishes.
In his overall conclusion, he evokes the Kabyle people who were
born, he argues, both to work and to be contemplative; they thus
had much to teach the 'anxious conquerors that we are' (*oc*, IV,
336). Camus was reflecting very much a liberal, minority position
within the European settler community although his clumsy talk
of 'anxious conquerors' draws attention, we might note, to the
subliminal fear that was part of the colonial mindset.

Critics have objected that much of the author's fictional work
reflects a cultural myopia. Thus in the early collection of essays

Nuptials, the beauty of Algerian landscapes is evoked often to the exclusion of the country's indigenous inhabitants (Tipasa and Djémila appear as marvellous landscapes with their local populations conspicuously absent). Yet there is a moment in 'Destitution in Kabylia' where Camus recognizes the risk of cultural blindness. It comes when he realizes, as the young journalist sitting up above the town of Tizi-Ouzou whose inhabitants are cold and hungry, that to be seduced by the natural beauty of the Kabyle setting is to ignore the human misery at hand (*oc*, IV, 311). In this note of caution, we see evidence of vigilance on Camus' part. Indeed his campaigning journalism, unlike his fictional work of the same period, was addressing directly the issue of social justice in colonial Algeria. Years later, in a memorial tribute to Camus, the Kabyle writer Mouloud Feraoun would cite specifically the moment of hesitation in 'Destitution in Kabylia' when Camus evoked the natural beauty of the evening in Kabylia but then checked himself, mindful of those starving close by: 'destitution here is not a mere form of words', Camus cautions, 'it places a prohibition on any talk of the beauty of the world' (*oc*, IV, 311).[14]

Camus was young and poor when he wrote those lines, Feraoun reflected, adding that in colonial Algeria he paid the price for his outspokenness. When the right-wing authorities in Algiers closed down *Le Soir Républicain* in January 1940, Camus found himself marginalized. As a young left-wing activist who had highlighted the economic consequences of colonial misrule, he was *persona non grata*. Earlier he had failed the army medical on health grounds at the outbreak of war in September 1939. He remained desperate to develop his career as a writer. After a brief spell in Oran where he gave some private classes teaching philosophy and pursued his relationship with Francine Faure, a young teacher of mathematics whom he had met in the autumn of 1937, he left for Paris in March 1940.

6

A Tale of Two Outsiders

Arriving in Paris to take up work was a big step for the young Camus after Algeria. He had visited the capital a few years earlier, recording enthusiastically his summer impressions: 'August 1937: Tenderness and emotion of Paris. The cats, the children, the relaxed ways of the people. The grey colours, the sky, a great parade of stone and waters' (*oc*, II, 823). March 1940 was a different proposition. Much later, in his 1958 preface for a new edition of *L'Envers et l'Endroit*, he would recall his horror on first discovering the working-class districts of France's industrial cities, adding that one could only feel diminished by the spectacle and responsible for such a state of affairs. Writing in openly sentimental terms, he suggested that the poverty he had experienced in his childhood was never a source of unhappiness. 'I was placed', he wrote, 'half way between poverty and the sun.' The result, he went on, was that poverty kept him from thinking that all was well with the world, while the light of the sun taught him another lesson, namely that 'history is not everything' (*oc*, I, 32).

Camus' target in his 1958 preface was the historicist view of the world which then held sway among left-wing French intellectuals. He knew that to reject historical materialism was an unfashionable move but he advanced a counter-argument, namely that climate and the natural environment had the capacity to inflict their own injustice. He conceded ironically that he would be provoking the wrath of left-wing commentators – 'our ferocious philanthropists' (*oc*, I, 33), as he labelled them – with an argument that seemed to say: pity the middle classes deprived of the sun and how lucky the workers of the south. His point, he stressed, was not to dismiss the materialist view of history but rather that when workers were poor and, in addition, living in France's ugly industrial suburbs, this represented a 'double humiliation' (*oc*, I, 33). Even the extreme destitution of the Arabs, because it was lived under another sky, he argued very contentiously, was not comparable to the degradation inflicted by the industrial suburbs of the north (*oc*, I, 33).

The greyness of Paris was what struck Camus when he arrived there in March 1940. It was the period of the 'phoney war', the lull before the rapid advance of the German army into northern France in May. He cut a solitary figure, spending his first few weeks in a rented room up in Montmartre. In Algiers he had been something of a Don Juan. He had also enjoyed being at the centre of a young cultural scene there, with his work in the theatre, journalism and the field of fiction meaning that he had a certain profile in the city.

For the move to Paris, Pascal Pia, his old boss from *Alger républicain* days, had managed to secure him work in the offices of the popular daily *Paris-Soir*, albeit in the mundane role of a *secrétaire de rédaction*, responsible for setting out the pages of the newspaper. Camus arrived in the capital on a Saturday and started on the Sunday. It was a clear step down from the responsibility he had enjoyed at *Alger républicain*. Moreover *Paris-Soir*, with its populist style, meant exposure to what he described as the city's abject outlook with its culture of 'sentimentalism and the picturesque' (*oc*, II, 913).

As a series of entries in his diary indicated, Camus felt uprooted: seen from Montmartre, the grey city below looked like a giant buoy under the incessant rain; a young woman on the floor above him threw herself to her death in the courtyard below; and in a restaurant he met a peasant refugee from Extremadura who, having fought on the Republican side in the Spanish Civil War, had now joined up with the French army. During a brief period of leave in the city, the soldier, with not a word of French, longed for human warmth. Camus absorbed these bleak images of desperation and yearning (*oc*, II, 908–11). In a handwritten amendment to the typescript of the *Carnets*, he was to tone down his pessimistic account of life in Paris, crossing out the line: 'this city is a terrible devourer of men.'[1]

The flatness of tone in the diary entries was to mirror the style of one of his most famous texts, *The Outsider*, which he had started work on back in 1937. In a letter to Christiane Galindo in July 1939, he indicated that he had a number of projects on the go: a play about the Emperor Caligula (which would eventually be performed in Paris in late September 1945); the novel *The Outsider*; and an essay, *The Myth of Sisyphus*, which he would go on to dedicate to Pascal Pia. Together, these three works would form the first phase in '[what] I am no longer afraid to call my work'.[2] This bundle of projects formed what Camus called the Cycle of the Absurd.

The routine of the working week at *Paris-Soir* was thus offset by what now most absorbed him, namely his writing. The Absurd was to become his trademark, the label indeed persisting long after his career and concerns as a writer had moved in new directions. As he explained in *The Myth of Sisyphus*, the Absurd involved the confrontation between man's awareness of his mortality and a world that remained altogether other and indifferent to human suffering. Talk of mortality was far from being an academic abstraction for Camus, who was no stranger to serious illness. In the human attachment to life, he saw a fundamental instinct: 'The judgement of the body is worth that of the mind', he protested, 'and the body recoils from the prospect of annihilation' (*oc*, I, 224). He mused that if he 'were a tree among trees, a cat among animals', he would not experience the alienation that came with the Absurd, with its 'fracture between the world and my mind' (*oc*, I, 254). *The Outsider* was to dramatize that sense of fracture.

Reviewing Sartre's novel of existential isolation, *La Nausée*, in *Alger républicain* back in October 1938, Camus had offered the rough-and-ready proposition that 'a novel is never anything other than a philosophy conveyed in images' (*oc*, I, 794). Around the same time he also read Sartre in the *Nouvelle Revue française* on the contemporary American novelists William Faulkner and John Dos Passos and their focus on the immediacy of everyday living. As if to echo this, the celebrated opening line of *The Outsider*, the 'aujourd'hui maman est morte' – 'My mother died today'[3] – throws the reader into a disarmingly concrete world and announces the first of three deaths. The second death, that of the Arab adversary whom the protagonist Meursault shoots on the beach at the end of Part I of the novel, paves the way for the third, with the impending execution of Meursault bringing the narrative to its conclusion. Camus was thus pulling together two narratives: one involving a son's allegedly callous indifference to the plight of his ageing mother; and the other a tale of homicide, with society exacting vengeance in the form of death by guillotine.

For over a year, Camus had been mulling over the strands that might feed into the novel but he was to write the bulk of the chapters quite quickly, between the time of his arrival in Paris in March 1940 and the beginning of May of that year, when he was able to inform Francine Faure back in Oran that he had completed a draft of the novel.

The subjects he had written about in the 1930s, notably in 'Summer in Algiers' and *The Wrong Side and the Right Side*, had provided a way in: the narrow outlook of the settler community of Algiers, the enigmatic silences between a mother and her son, a generational divide that saw the elderly isolated, and a street culture marked by male bravado and aggression. This last element is conspicuous in *The Outsider* where the misogynist Raymond

Sintès, who draws Meursault into the spiral of violence that leads to the killing of a North African on the beach, has his face slapped by a policeman for casually continuing to draw on his cigarette as he is questioned. The depiction of a culture of machismo is as much a part of *The Outsider* as the visceral protest against the state's recourse to the violence of the guillotine.

How a novel which would become Gallimard's all-time best-selling paperback and be translated into over 50 languages found its way into print is itself an important story. Pascal Pia was to be pivotal in securing the work's acceptance. Writing in late March 1941 to Camus, who was then in Oran, he asked him to forward him the manuscript. Pia was unreservedly positive about what he read and had the work sent on to the novelist André Malraux, who was a figure of considerable influence. Malraux made numerous constructive suggestions for stylistic reworking. Camus acted on these and at the same time assuaged some doubts expressed by his mentor Jean Grenier, who felt there was the risk of an unhelpful echo of Kafka in the novel. Well able to assume the respectful role of the apprentice, Camus replied that the characters and episodes of his novel were perhaps more grounded in a concrete everyday world than those in the work of Kafka.

Ironically, the author of this future best-seller had been beset with self-doubt. Crucially, Camus had been keen to know from Grenier if he thought it worth his while persisting in his attempts to be a writer. This was back in June 1938 when Camus, who was generally fairly guarded about such questions, had written to Grenier, asking: 'Do you sincerely believe I should continue writing? I ask myself this question with much anxiety.' Camus expressed his embarrassment at being so direct (as we saw earlier, he was temperamentally quite at home with the 'muted and [the] unformulated' (*oc*, IV, 1285)). Yet as he explained to Jean Grenier, for two years he had been mulling these doubts over in isolation. He stressed that it was not the advantages of a professional career that he was seeking: 'I don't have that many pure things in my life. Writing is one of them.'[4] By November 1941 Grenier had good news: Gallimard had accepted *The Outsider* for publication. A first print run of 4,400 copies in May 1942 would be followed by similar-sized print runs six months and twelve months later.

Some autobiographical elements filtered through to *The Outsider*. Camus' work as an office temp in a shipping agent's was one of them. At a more sombre level, Meursault's visceral protest against the death penalty triggers memories of how his father, years before, returned home to be physically sick from what he had seen. This image of a body in shock drew on Camus' own father's experience of having gone to witness a public execution at the Barberousse Prison in Algiers in the expectation of seeing justice done and yet being nauseated by the spectacle. Camus knew little about his father but the latter's haunting memory of the spectacle of public execution remained one of the salient elements in that patchy life history. Little wonder that Lucien Camus' revulsion at the guillotine provides the opening for Camus' essay *Réflexions sur la guillotine* (Reflections on the Guillotine), which came out in 1957. In Camus' novel, Meursault in prison is troubled by the cold mechanics of the guillotine, which exemplifies what in *The Myth of Sisyphus* Camus refers to as 'the bloody mathematics which orders our human condition' (*oc*, I, 230).

In Camus' case the borders between life and fiction were porous. He was to be an active campaigner against the death penalty in the 1950s, making numerous pleas for clemency in a wide range of cases – Spanish, Tunisian, Greek, Hungarian, Iranian and Vietnamese. And during the Algerian War, when the French government made widespread use of the death penalty against Algerian insurrectionaries, Camus privately made an estimated 150 appeals for clemency.[5]

The Outsider was Camus' first published novel. He had left unfinished an earlier novel, *La Mort heureuse* (A Happy Death), which would appear posthumously in 1971. A story of the quest for happiness of its young protagonist Patrice Mersault, *A Happy Death* lacked the tightness of focus that in *The Outsider* carries the narrative through to its melodramatic denouement.

As an enthusiastic reader of Guilloux's *La Maison du peuple* in his late teens, Camus had detected in that novel's compositional style a principle of understatement. He recorded in his notebooks in 1938 that 'the real work of art is the one that says less.' *The Outsider* saw him put the prescription into action. Its muted, often flat tone matches Meursault's understated character. The novel records in pared-down fashion a series of events with little attention paid to establishing a justificatory framing for them.[6]

In a brief essay which appeared in the Lyons-based journal *Confluences* in July 1943, 'L'Intelligence et L'Echafaud' (Intelligence and the Scaffold), Camus gave a punchy definition of how prose composition worked by likening the French classical novelist pursuing a narrative thread to the executioner whose task is to bring the condemned to his punishment without deviation or digression. In particular he hailed the sense of economy in the work of Madame de Lafayette and other French novelists. For them, art acts like 'a form of revenge' (*OC*, 1, 900) by giving taut aesthetic form to a difficult fate.

How *The Outsider* fared in the hands of successive generations of readers tells its own cultural and social history and has a bearing on our biographical understanding of Camus. For a number of years after its publication, the novel was read as highlighting universal questions without reference to the specificity of colonial Algeria. Sartre's *explication* or explanation of the novel in the *Nouvelle Revue française* in February 1943 was foundational in this respect. His review set out the links between the dilemma facing Sisyphus and the situation of Meursault and rehearsed the Camusian notion of the Absurd, restating the confrontation between man's aspiration to life and the knowledge of his finite

ALBERT CAMUS

L'Étranger

roman

nrf

GALLIMARD

Front cover of the first edition of *L'Etranger* (1942). The novel would be translated into over 50 languages.

existence. But his reading of the work was strikingly Eurocentric and he referred exotically to the book as a stranger of a novel that brought a touch of Mediterranean sun 'in this bitter spring without coal' (the reference was to wartime fuel shortages).[7] Sartre positioned the work culturally in Europe, referring to the tradition of moralist fiction *à la* Voltaire, the moralism of Pascal and the pessimistic worldview of Dostoyevsky. Indeed the absence of connection with colonial Algeria in Sartre's review remains striking. Remarkably there is only the most fleeting reference to

Meursault's killing of his Arab adversary. Sartre writes bizarrely that the work feels less like a novel than 'a monotonous chant, [the] nasal song of an Arab'.[8] The specificity of life in colonial Algiers is thus lost behind exoticist cliché.

The virtual exclusion of North Africa from Sartre's review of 1943 is all the more surprising given that there are strong local currents in *The Outsider* which make the novel as much about Algeria as it is about the Absurd. Suspicion between the European and indigenous communities was deep-seated and the Algiers press in the summer of 1939 carried coverage of murder stories involving the consumption of alcohol, intense heat and inter-ethnic violence. As a journalist then working for *Alger républicain* whose remit included legal cases, Camus was familiar with courtroom life in the city.[9]

In the light of this strong historical contextualization, it is ironic to look back on the verdict of the wartime German censors who deemed the work apolitical and asocial.[10] In later years and for other readers, it was to be a different story. In a private letter to the young historian Pierre Nora in April 1961, Jacques Derrida complained that Sartre's 'critico-philosophical' reading of *The Outsider* in 1943 had stripped the text of its historical meaning and originality and inclined Camus to see the text in a similar light. In his counter-argument, namely that *The Outsider* was first and foremost an Algerian novel, Derrida was endorsing Nora's view that the scene of homicide in the novel gave expression to the unconscious desire of the settler to be rid of the colonized.[11]

Derrida's letter had been prompted by Nora's trenchant book *Les Français d'Algérie* (The French Algerians), written after its young metropolitan author had spent two years teaching in Oran during the Algerian War. The book was published in March 1961 at a time when the future of Algeria hung in the balance (the following month saw a French military putsch aimed at arresting the slide towards Algerian independence). For Nora,

The Outsider was the only great work of literature to have come out of a culture which he characterized as being 'consciously frozen in historical immobility'.[12] In Meursault, the office clerk with no ambition, Nora saw an embodiment of the narrow horizons that for him were a hallmark of the French Algerian mentality. He seized on the fact that Camus had been living in Oran, something of a cultural backwater, before heading off to Paris in March 1940. In Nora's words, not only must Oran have made Camus feel like Robinson Crusoe on his desert island but, he went on caustically, there was a Crusoe trapped within every French Algerian.[13]

Nora would later write influentially about the phenomenon of a community's will to construct and remember its heritage through the creation of *lieux de mémoire* (sites of memory). In his *Les Français d'Algérie*, he had seen Camus not just as a figure of the Left, the journalist at *Alger républicain* who had filed the reports that made up 'Destitution in Kabylia', but as a writer whose work captures that 'moment when the French felt their domination to be contested'.[14] *The Outsider*, for Nora, thus charted in fictional form the latent aggression in the settler mindset. Edward Said would later argue that resituating the text colonially was to 'interpret it as a heightened form of historical experience'.[15]

When one looks across from Sartre's early reading of Meursault as the naive Sancho Panza of the Absurd to Nora's categorization of *The Outsider* as a repository for the colonial unconscious, the spectrum of response is wide.[16] If the intense exposure received over decades by *The Outsider* forms part of the text's vigorous afterlife, it is worth contrasting this with the obscure circumstances in which its author, as a 26-year-old writer largely unknown in Paris, composed the work. He was living in a rented room in the spring of 1940, working on an uninspiring newspaper and finding the capital unattractive. Weeks after he had completed his draft of the novel, the 'phoney war' came to an end. With the prospect of an invading German army arriving in Paris, Camus, who had been very much an outsider when he arrived in the capital from Algeria just over three months earlier, now prepared to join the mass movement of population towards the south. He would take with him in the boot of the car in which he was travelling the draft manuscript of *The Outsider*.

7

'All Man's Misery . . .'

Camus' first spell working in Paris thus came to an abrupt end in early June 1940 when, with the Nazi occupation of the capital imminent – the Germans entered the city on 14 June – *Paris-Soir* hastily relocated. It transferred its operation to Clermont-Ferrand, then to Bordeaux, then back to Clermont, and eventually to Lyons in September. The months of May–June 1940 saw the military collapse of France. *La débâcle*, as it came to be known, was a period of utter social collapse. As the populations of northern cities took to the roads in an attempt to escape the advancing German army, Camus now joined the exodus formed of an estimated six to ten million people, their numbers swollen by refugees from the Low Countries heading south.[1]

Under the terms of the armistice signed with Germany on 22 June 1940, France was divided up. A zone in the north came under direct occupation by the German army, while to the south, an Unoccupied Zone, centred around Vichy, was established. Here, French rule was retained, although with a government that was obliged to negotiate with the occupying power. Camus, in the wake of the exodus from Paris, was now living in that southern zone. He felt hemmed in not just physically, but ideo-logically, in the highly claustrophobic world of the Unoccupied Zone.[2] The 85-year-old Marshal Pétain was installed there as collaborationist Head of State in July 1940. Anti-Semitism was rife in Vichy France.

Stranded and desperate to get back to Algeria, the young Camus wrote sombrely to his fiancée Francine Faure, who was on the other side of the Mediterranean in Oran, that 'cowardice and senility' had taken over in France.[3] Significantly however, the disarray brought about by the war did not halt Camus' work as a writer and his pursuit of his artistic vocation remained tenacious. We thus find some of the manuscript of *The Myth of Sisyphus*, for example, written on paper bearing the letter-head *Paris-Soir*, 57 rue Blatin, Clermont-Ferrand. The address was that of the regional newspaper *Le Moniteur* whose premises had been made available to *Paris-Soir* and other Parisian papers when they were migrated south by its owner, the politician Pierre Laval, who was to become Vichy's Head of Government in 1942.

Camus was joined in Lyons in late November 1940 by Francine, who travelled over from Oran. Earlier that year, his divorce from Simon Hié had come through. As an aspiring writer living in Algeria in the late 1930s, he had had numerous girlfriends and in a letter to one of them, Christiane Galindo, on 25 July 1939, he had wondered if settling down was really for him: 'For my work I need mental freedom and freedom full stop.'[4] He was uninhibited sexually, evoking in his diary in July 1937 'the warm beast of desire that one carries in one's loins and which stirs with a ferocious sweetness' (*oc*, II, 822). By casting Tirso de Molina's character Don Juan as a heroic figure in his *The Myth of Sisyphus*, Camus found a literary exemplar to reflect this libertarian outlook: Don Juan embodied the will to love and to do so without restriction. By contrast, Francine Faure, a teacher from a cultured middle-class Oran family, saw things more conventionally. They were married on 3 December 1940 in a low-key affair, with Pascal Pia as a witness and a few of Camus' friends from the newspaper also present. As one of the guests later enthused, 'I found it moving, their getting married in such a simple way, with three or four of us typesetters making up the wedding party.'[5]

Yet within a matter of days, Camus had lost his job when *Paris-Soir*, its circulation falling, laid off staff. With little money coming in, the newlyweds were forced to return to Oran where they stayed in the rue d'Arzew in accommodation provided by Francine's family.

Francine had not married a Nobel Prize winner. While she worked as a supply teacher, he had no fixed employment. On the writing front, he continued to nudge forward, completing a draft of *The Myth of Sisyphus* by February 1941. When he brought out the work with Gallimard in October 1942, it appeared only after he had excised the appended essay on the Jewish writer Kafka, the intention being to avoid attracting the attention of the wartime censors (Camus published his Kafka piece separately in the clandestine review *L'Arbalète* in Lyons in the summer of 1943).

The impact of the politics of Vichy was clearly visible in the Oran of 1941, which had the highest concentration of Jews of any Algerian town. Anti-Semitic legislation had seen the withdrawal of civil rights from the Jewish population in Algeria with the abrogation in October 1940 of the Crémieux Decree of 1870, which had given French citizenship to the country's Jews. Thus Camus' friend from schooldays André Bénichou, a lycée teacher in Oran, found himself stripped of his post. Over 26,000 Jews and their children in the town were now assigned to the category of former French citizens.[6] Camus did some occasional teaching in private institutions set up to cater for the Jewish children excluded from the state system.

Unsurprisingly the themes of encirclement and imprisonment were to feature prominently in his writing during the war and among the works he took forward in that period were the play *Le Malentendu* (The Misunderstanding) and his second novel, *The Plague*. The setting for the carceral atmosphere of the novel was the town of Oran, where Camus lived for much of 1941 and the first half of 1942. He wrote from there to Jean Grenier on 28 July 1941 about the sense of loneliness induced by the town, which he likened to 'a wild and baking-hot labyrinth'. Oran was a 'desert without an oasis', a place that awoke a need to reconnect with civilization.[7]

The Plague opens with an unflattering depiction of the town built with its back to the sea: 'How can one convey, for example', the narrator asks, 'the idea of a town without pigeons, without trees or gardens . . .? In summer the sun burns the dried-out houses and covers their walls with grey powder.'[8] An outbreak of typhoid in Algeria in July 1941 was to feed into Camus' preparatory work for the novel and in October he began researching the subject of historical and literary accounts of plague epidemics, among them Daniel Defoe's *A Journal of the Plague Year* (1722). An epidemic carried on board a ship was a theme in Melville's *Moby Dick* and Camus' diary entries of the period show this providing further preparatory material for his project.

The year 1942 brought him mixed fortunes. May saw the publication of *The Outsider* in Paris, but before that he suffered a relapse of tuberculosis in February and was obliged to rest. His economic situation thus became all the more precarious. 'Sickness and Oran, that makes two deserts', he complained to Jean Grenier. A fortnight later, on 7 March 1942, he wrote with resignation, 'For the moment, I am inactive in the most indifferent city in the world.'[9] Camus was advised on health grounds to rest and to live at semi-altitude. In August he and Francine travelled from Algeria to Le Panelier, a hamlet close to Le Chambon-sur-Lignon up in the hills above Saint-Etienne in the Vivarais region. A relative of Francine's ran a guest house there. While Francine had to return to her teaching in Oran in the autumn, Camus stayed on in the Massif Central. And when Allied troops invaded Algeria in November 1942, he was effectively cut off from his family in North Africa. He and Francine were to be separated for much of the rest of the war and it was not until October 1944 that they were reunited in Paris as the Liberation of France progressed.

The experience of the war saw Camus' connection with metropolitan France gradually deepen. He confided in a letter to Jean Grenier sent from Le Panelier on 9 March 1943 that he had come to appreciate what *la patrie* (the fatherland) meant, although he added that it was not to his honour that it had taken much suffering for him to get to that point of connection.[10] In the same letter, he explained that he had been busy with his writing and conveyed a mood of withdrawal, citing John Henry Newman's exhortation to 'admire the things of this world at the moment we renounce it'.[11] Camus' periodic relapses into serious illness contributed to this outlook and in a letter of August 1943 to the Resistance poet Francis Ponge he wrote of being divided 'between Paris and my health, between my dislike of being in France and the sense of obligation to remain here. I hope that work will save me from all of this.'[12] He was to channel this tension between solitude and social solidarity into his fiction. It was in December 1943 that he committed actively to the work of the Resistance.

In his 'Lettres à un ami allemand' (Letters to a German Friend), a series of four letters to an imagined German correspondent, Camus characterized the individual's attitude to the nation as something complex. Three of the letters appeared in clandestine publications in Occupied France, the first of them in *La Revue libre* in July 1943 (*OC*, II, 1129). In that opening exchange, the imagined German interlocutor chides the author of the letter for wanting to love both his country and justice – in the mind of the German friend, this reflected an ambiguous stance and betrayed a lack of patriotism. The retort of the French correspondent is that 'this country merits the complex and demanding love that is mine' (*OC*, II, 13). For Camus, subjecting both the attachment to nation and the recourse to war to scrutiny was the necessary counter to blind acceptance of state propaganda. In short, scrutiny was the antidote to totalitarianism.

But lyricism was also part of Camus' armoury in his response to Fascism in 'Letters to a German Friend'. He complained that for five years 'it has no longer been possible to enjoy the cries of birds in the cool evening air' (*oc*, ii, 27). He warned nevertheless that history's bloody incursion would be thwarted by nature. In a tone reminiscent of the patriotic Maurice Barrès from an earlier generation of French writers, Camus vaunted the power of the national soil to become reborn and predicted that 'the obstinacy of the returns of spring' made victory inevitable (*oc*, ii, 23).

During the period of the war when he stayed at Le Panelier, Camus regularly bicycled down to Saint-Etienne for his medical treatment. He reacted viscerally to the drabness of the working-class town where 'everyone was dressed in black',[13] and some years later, in 1955, on a visit to the ancient site of Tipasa on the Algerian coast, he returned to the theme of the miserable lives of those born in France's industrial towns. 'How lucky to be born on the hills of Tipasa', he insisted, 'and not in Saint-Etienne or Roubaix' (*oc*, iv, 1220). He described life up in Le Panelier as monastic with its 'austerity, silence, solitude'.[14] 'History is turned upside down', he wrote to Grenier, 'but everyday life (*la petite vie*) carries on'.[15] From the Massif Central in February 1943, he posted a packet of books to his mentor, asking him to leave all the packaging material (the string included) with an actor friend of his in Paris, Paul Oettly, in whose mother's guest house back in Le Panelier Camus was staying. A food parcel sent to the Greniers a few months later contained goat's cheese with advice from Camus on how to freshen it up (brief immersion in water) and some mushroom powder which he had prepared from ceps he had gathered in the woods.

The landlocked world of the Massif Central also provided the backdrop to Camus' work on *The Misunderstanding*. The play picked up on a news item that he had originally come across in the Algiers press in early 1935 and that he had featured in the storyline of *The Outsider*, where Meursault in his prison cell keeps a newspaper cutting with a dramatic story of misrecognition. A man returning home to central Europe after twenty years spent living in a Mediterranean country chooses to remain incognito and books into the drab hotel run by his family. During the night his mother and sister kill him (their plan being to enrich themselves and thus escape to the Mediterranean, where they long to be). Their discovery of his true identity the following day drives them both to suicide.

The play hinges on the opposition between a central European location portrayed as grey and soulless and a more southerly space seen as a place of liberation. Jean Grenier, who regularly gave Camus feedback on his manuscript drafts, found Martha, the sister of the returning son, the play's most compelling character. More to the point, he saw Camus in her. 'I am too far from what I love', she asserts, 'and nothing can remedy that distance' (*oc*, I, 491). Martha also complains that she has been 'buried away in the heart of the continent . . . I grew up inland within its thick folds' (*oc*, I, 489). By February 1943, Camus was writing to Grenier with a similar

At the premises of the 'Secours National' in wartime Saint-Etienne, meals are served to the needy. Camus was outspoken about living conditions for the working class in France's industrial cities.

complaint: he had had enough of the grey skies and snow-covered roads of the Massif Central. 'Never before have I thought so much about light and heat. This really is exile.'[16] His sense of isolation and geographical dislocation midway through the Second World War was stark and something of that desperation filters through to the strained words of Martha: 'However much I may press my ear to the earth, I shall not hear the sound of the icy waves breaking or the measured breathing of the happy sea' (*oc*, I, 491). If the contrasting ecologies of France's Massif Central and Algeria were keenly felt by Camus, Martha gave voice to that sense of exile.

The war also shaped the moral climate of *The Misunderstanding*, which carries a reflection on violence, wrongdoing and individual responsibility. The fratricidal Martha sees her crime as condemning her to isolation: 'crime too is a solitude even if one becomes part of a thousand-strong group to accomplish it' (*oc*, I, 495), she ponders darkly. And her mother reflects that whereas the killing of guests had become routine for her, it had taken the return of her son to re-sensitize her to the reality of their serial killing: 'The experience of pain was enough to transform everything' (*oc*, I, 488), she reveals.

The reflections on the banality of killing and on the re-emergence of moral angst, while they risked exposing the play to the charge that it was mere thesis drama, were to anticipate the urgent social debates that became increasingly prominent as the war came to an end. Already in 'Letters to a German Friend', as we have seen, Camus was busy bringing an urgent moral tone to the debate.

He had submitted the manuscripts for both *Caligula* and *The Misunderstanding* to Gallimard in October 1943 and in the following May a joint edition of the plays, both of which were to be subsequently modified, appeared. Camus dedicated the volume to 'My Friends in the Théâtre de l'Equipe' with whom he had worked back in Algiers in the mid-1930s.

In late 1943 Camus left central France for Paris. In November he took up a position with the publisher Gallimard as a professional reader of book proposals, becoming a member of their Comité de lecture (Readers' Committee). Around the same time, Pascal Pia introduced him to the Resistance group responsible for producing and distributing the clandestine newspaper *Combat*, which in August of the following year, with the Liberation of Paris, would become one of the principal organs of the newly liberated press.

In the spring of 1944 preparations began for the staging of *The Misunderstanding* at the Théâtre des Mathurins in Paris where Marcel Herrand was director. Cast in the role of Martha was a 21-year-old actress who was to become Camus' lover, the young Maria Casares. In her autobiography she recalled their first meeting as an experience of instant connection. She sensed in him, she wrote, a powerful searching, 'the mad intensity of which shines in the eyes of Goya's characters', except that in Camus' case she found it to be tightly held in check. Casares exuberantly suggested that 'had he been a doctor and I the patient, he would have only had to appear for me to feel better'.[17] She enthused about his 'vitality, passion, imagination, commitment to individual liberty of thought and speech'.[18]

Maria Casares had been born into a prominent Spanish Republican family and her father, Santiago Casares Quiroga, had been prime minister of the country in 1936 until the outbreak of the Spanish Civil War on 17 July. Spanishness was an important ingredient in the chemistry between her and Camus and she saw in him a kindred spirit in exile. As an immigrant in France having fled Franco's Spain, she was to become a leading figure in post-war French theatre and cinema, appearing for example in Marcel Carné's *Les Enfants du Paradis* in 1945 and Cocteau's *Orphée* (1949).

When *The Misunderstanding* was premiered at the Théâtre des Mathurins on 23 June 1944 in front of an invited audience, it was met with a hostile reception.[19] The awkwardness in parts of the dialogue and some predictable elements of plot were ridiculed. There was the added suggestion that Camus' lack of sympathy for the collaborationist press inclined many of the journalists present to vent their hostility. Yet in spite of the first-night boos and whistles, a defiant Casares in the role of Martha kept going to the end, breaking down with the emotion and effort of it all only after the final curtain.[20] That summer, with the Allied invasion of Normandy in early June 1944, the course of the war was set to change and a month after the opening night of *The Misunderstanding*, the play's run was suspended, to be resumed only for a two-week period in October.

The fate of Nazi collaborators was now set to become a burning question and talk of guilt, retribution and responsibility was everywhere. While Martha on the set of *The Misunderstanding* at the Théâtre des Mathurins in July was submitting herself to the law of a rigorous morality – 'it is right that I die alone having lived and killed alone' (*oc*, I, 495) – Camus was adopting a no less declamatory tone in his journalism. An anonymous article probably authored by him in what was the still-clandestine *Combat* in July 1944 carried the headline 'Vous serez jugés sur vos actes' (You will be judged by your actions).[21] Commenting on the collaborationist roles of Pétain and Pierre Laval, the article struck a note of moral intransigence. And just as in *The Misunderstanding* 'plain language' was needed to break the murderous cycle, so France, the article insisted, needed 'courage and clear language'. The stress on individual responsibility within collective violence was to be a key element in that moral debate.

While Camus' own outlook remained a secular one, the experience of working alongside a number of Christians during the Second World War allowed him to appreciate what he saw as their moral probity. These contacts did not go unnoticed: his Communist friend Francis Ponge confessed to feeling uneasy about the link to religion. Yet Camus was unrepentant, arguing that for those deeply committed in their religious beliefs, 'I have more than sympathy, I feel linked to them in solidarity.'[22]

René Leynaud was one such figure. A poet and journalist working for the newspaper *Le Progrès de Lyon*, he had been a member of the Resistance from early 1942. He and Camus met in Saint-Etienne when Camus was living in Le Panelier and they met again in the spring of 1944 in Paris. In October that year news emerged that Leynaud, who had been arrested in Lyons in May by local militias, had been shot dead by the Gestapo on 13 June along with eighteen other prisoners in a wood near Villeneuve. Camus paid tribute to him in *Combat* (27 October 1944) and dedicated *Letters to a German Friend* to his memory when Gallimard brought out an edition of the work a year later.

The emotion of wartime loss was filtering through into *The Plague*, much of which was composed against the backdrop of the Occupation and the Liberation. While on the surface the novel chronicled the impact of bubonic plague in Oran, its allegorical character allowed its post-war readers when the work appeared in 1947 to make the link to the experience of Nazi Occupation, known in France as 'la peste brune' or 'the brown plague' (the reference being to the colour of the shirts worn by the occupying army). When Bernard Rieux, the doctor, sees his friend Tarrou succumb to the disease at the very time when the epidemic is ending, he realizes that there can be no peace for him personally, 'any more than there is an armistice for the mother amputated from her son or for the man who buries his friend'.[23]

The death of René Leynaud was one such amputation for Camus. In a *Combat* editorial of 27 October 1944, Leynaud was singled out for his moral integrity and sacrifice, Camus stressing that the poet had forgone his art to commit to the war (*oc*, ii, 411). Camus also provided a preface for the publication of Leynaud's *Poésies posthumes* (Posthumous Poetry, 1947) in which he confessed that in his 30 years of life, 'never has the death of a man so reverberated within me' (*oc*, ii, 710). Mindful of Leynaud's religious conviction, Camus wrote emotionally that his friend now belonged to 'that other thing that had no meaning for me and . . . the only place where I could not join him was his certainty. But he loved my difference as I loved his' (*oc*, II, 710).

Camus had not gone soft on religion. (A few years later, in his new play *L'Etat de siège* (State of Siege), first performed in Paris's Marigny Theatre in October 1948, he excoriated totalitarian government in Franco's Spain, prompting the Catholic writer Gabriel Marcel to protest against the 'burlesque and odious light' in which religion was represented in the play.[24]) He was temperamentally not uncomfortable with talk of moral integrity and his work on *The Plague* was allowing him to develop the voice of the moralist. A keen reader of Blaise Pascal, he would later refer to the author of the *Pensées* as 'the greatest of all, yesterday and today'. The poet Jacques Roubaud would reinforce the connection, astutely likening Camus to 'a secular Pascal'.[25]

An echo of Pascal's famous dictum that 'All man's woes derive from one thing, his inability to remain quietly in a room' was present in Camus' remark of January 1946 to Louis Guilloux about the source of tragedy in *The Misunderstanding*: 'all man's misery stems from the fact that he does not know how to use a simple language' (concretely in the case of the play: had the returning son explained who he was, tragedy would have been averted).[26] Later in his career he would paraphrase Pascal's dictum: writing in *The Rebel* about 'the sons of Cain', he argued that 'All the miseries of men derive from the hope which tears them away from the silence of the citadel and throws them on to the ramparts in the expectation of salvation' (*oc*, III, 85).

8

Combat and the Narrative of Liberation

Lucidity, refusal, persistence, irony.
Camus on 'the four commandments of journalism'[1]

With the Liberation of Paris in August 1944, *Combat* ceased
to be a clandestine publication. Now operating in the rue
Réaumur out of the former premises of the *Pariser Zeitung*
(the newspaper of the German Occupation Forces in Paris),
it had become a daily with a circulation that was to peak at
200,000 copies. Four years earlier the 26-year-old Camus had
arrived in Paris from Algeria to take up a humdrum job as a
sub-editor at *Paris-Soir*. Now as chief editor of *Combat*, he was
a high-profile journalist speaking to the nation. Just as the
recently founded *Le Monde* was seen as the paper of Hubert
Beuve-Méry, so readers saw *Combat* as Camus' paper.[2] In the
twelve months following the launch of the new format, he was
a prolific contributor to its pages.

   With Resistance fighters attacking German targets in the city,
the battle for Paris was raging when the new *Combat* was launched
on 21 August 1944. In its first editorial, entitled 'Le Combat
continue . . .' (The battle goes on . . .), Camus wrote: 'After fifty
months of occupation, struggles and sacrifices, Paris is reborn to
the feeling of liberty' (*CAC*, 139–40). A few days later, with fighting
in the capital continuing, he rallied his readers: 'Today Paris fights
so that tomorrow France may speak' (*CAC*, 149).

Front cover of *Combat*, 24 August 1944.

Camus' interventions as a wielder of words were part of a grand narrative of the people's liberation and the talk in the paper was of national reconstruction on a revolutionary scale. His early editorials contained high-flown appeals to freedom, truth and the emotion of contempt. Reviewing the state of the press in two articles that appeared on 31 August and 1 September 1944, Camus wrote of how the pre-war press had been in the grip of big finance and he called for political moves to free journalism from the influence of capital. The responsibility of journalists towards their reading public had to be restored, he insisted, in the wake of the years of Fascist collaboration. In his signed articles the tone was unequivocally moral, as were the paper's anonymous editorials, many of which can be attributed to him. 'Politics and morality are interdependent' (*CAC*, 163), he announced unambiguously on 1 September. He went a step further three days later, writing of a revolutionary resolve to replace politics with morality (*CAC*, 171). In this moral turn, Camus was signalling a style of political pronouncement that would be a hallmark of the public interventions he was to make throughout the rest of his career.

Combat reflected the views of the non-Communist left. It aimed to represent workers' interests and the pursuit of that end was expressed in strongly aspirational terms: 'We believe that any politics that separates itself from the working class is futile. Tomorrow France will be what its working class will be' (*CAC*, 143), read an editorial attributed to Camus of 21 August 1944. He likewise dismissed the populist press, advocating instead 'a daily effort of reflection and scrupulousness' (*CAC*, 165). In another leader attributed to him (6 September 1944), readers were reminded of how the French bourgeoisie had rallied to Vichy in order to exact revenge on Léon Blum's Popular Front government,which had been elected in 1936 (*CAC*, 171–2).

With the Liberation came the inevitable settling of scores and Camus was initially forthright in supporting the policy of purging

– *l'épuration* – in the cases of 'those [collaborators] prominent in the fields of industry and thought' (*CAC*, 264). The leading car manufacturer Louis Renault, for example, was the focus of an editorial of 26 September 1944 (Renault had been arrested but died before his case came to trial). The editorial argued that in cases of such flagrant collaboration, 'there should be no shame in saying that the accusation is moral and irrefutable' (*CAC*, 208).

In October 1944 Camus clashed with the Catholic writer François Mauriac on the merit of the moral case for the purges. Mauriac, writing in the conservative *Le Figaro* and calling for the Christian virtue of charity to be exercised, urged clemency whereas Camus argued that some pardons were impossible. France must be capable of achieving, he insisted, both 'its victory and its truth' (*CAC*, 276). To that end, he appealed to 'the notion of national indignity' (*CAC*, 266) as a necessary tool in the work of reconstruction while also expressing the view that the purges should be effective and brought to a swift conclusion.

Mauriac was no less tenacious in his defence of the principle of Christian love. He dismissed his opponent as 'our young master (*maître*) who has bright ideas about every subject'.[3] Not one to turn the other cheek, Camus reacted strongly to Mauriac's paternalistic tone, rejecting his view that Christ had died for the whole of mankind: 'Monsieur Mauriac hurls Christ in my face', he objected, adding that 'a divine charity would rob men of their justice' (*CAC*, 441–2).

Yet *Combat*'s chief editor, who indeed would later become an outspoken opponent of the death penalty, quickly became disillusioned with the manner in which the purge trials were being conducted. The high-profile case of the writer Robert Brasillach troubled him. Brasillach had been an ardent supporter of the Nazis and had written for the pro-Nazi newspaper *Je suis partout* (I am everywhere). He was sentenced to death in January 1945. When a petition seeking clemency was launched, Camus, having initially refused to sign, gave his backing after much soul-searching. Yet Brasillach was executed, De Gaulle refusing to be swayed by the appeal. By late August 1945 a disillusioned Camus would publicly state that the practice of *l'épuration* had been a failure and he went on to concede that Mauriac had been right (*OC*, II, 471).[4]

In the spring of 1945 Camus' work for *Combat* took him to Algeria. The trip served as a painful reminder of how intensely volatile the situation was in the colony. He covered a considerable distance between 18 April and 7–8 May, not only visiting the coastal region but driving down to the southern part of the Constantinois region and visiting Kabylia. As it happened, his trip came to an end just before the eruption of major violence in the country.

8 May 1945 saw the end of the war in Europe. It coincided with an Algerian revolt in the areas of Sétif and Guelma in which over a hundred European settlers were massacred. In retaliatory action involving French air and marine artillery strikes, thousands of Algerians were killed. With Camus by that stage back in Paris, his reports in *Combat* did not offer detailed, on-the-ground coverage of the violence but rather focused on the socio-economic crisis facing the country.

Months earlier, however, in a *Combat* editorial of 13 October 1944, he had sounded a note of caution on the question of colonial politics. His advice then had been that as a colonial power, metropolitan France, having lost prestige in the eyes of native Algerians in the course of the Second World War, needed to resist any temptation to flex its muscles in the colony. Warning against the dangers of militarism, Camus called for the need to avoid a politics that 'would give justice to the people of France and another that would sanction injustice in its Empire' (*CAC*, 253). Subsequent bloody events would underscore the pertinence of that earlier editorial. The brutal severity of the French military reprisals in Sétif and Guelma came to form a watershed moment in France's colonial relations in Algeria. With hindsight some Algerians came to see the massive loss of life in May 1945 as the beginning of the Algerian War. That was certainly the view of Kateb Yacine, who witnessed Sétif and would go on to become a prominent writer. Yet if he saw Sétif as the moment when his Algerian nationalist conviction took shape, the story of the bloody reprisals was covered up in France. Simone de Beauvoir noted in her auto-biography that the Communist newspaper *L'Humanité* had set the level of casualties at about a hundred.[5]

With the situation critical in May 1945, Camus was desperately seeking to inject urgency into metropolitan thinking on Algeria. He advocated reform, warning that this was 'the last chance that France has of saving its future in North Africa' (*CAC*, 529). He brought to the attention of his metropolitan readership the political work of Ferhat Abbas, commending as 'a key figure of remarkable ability' the head of the moderate nationalist movement formed with the establishment of the Amis du Manifeste (Friends of the Manifesto) in 1943. He urged his French readers to take the movement seriously since it had 'entered deeply into Arab political aspirations' (*CAC*, 527).

Camus was also exercised by the stream of misinformation being channelled through the French press. A week earlier (13–14 May 1945), he had reported finding in the most remote tribal villages, 800 kilometres from the coast, Muslim inhabitants out-raged by the suggestion in the French press that the unrest in Algeria was the work of demagogues inciting the simple-minded to violence (*CAC*, 500).[6] This anecdotal evidence gleaned in the country's *douars* allowed Camus to appreciate the extent of political awakening within what he termed 'the Muslim masses'. He could see that the calls in the right-wing French press for repres-sive measures would only exacerbate matters (*CAC*, 502).

Camus was also outspoken about the political leanings of the settler community. As he reminded his *Combat* readers, the politics of Vichy were nowhere more avidly espoused than in colonial

Algeria, especially in its reactionary press (*Alger républicain*, where he had worked, and to a lesser extent *Oran républicain* being exceptions in this regard). 'Democracy does not have a good press in Algeria', he cautioned, singling out the country's business and financial elites together with high-ranking civil servants in the Government General as being among the most reactionary political elements. He reminded his readers how, back in 1938, it was wealthy colonialists and the Association of the Mayors of Algeria that had scuppered the very modest reform plan of the French government to enfranchise a small number of Algerians, the so-called Blum-Viollette proposals (*CAC*, 516).

Camus' May 1945 *Combat* reports on Algeria were thus intended as a wake-up call. Desperate to remedy the metropolitan ignorance of life there, he asked his readers if they wished to be 'hated by millions of men'. To avoid such a situation, Camus urged his readers to welcome the people of North Africa as their equals (*CAC*, 532). As with his June 1939 work on the subject of famine in Kabylia immediately before the Second World War, his reporting from Algeria as the war drew to an end came with a call for radical economic reform.

A visit in late June 1945 to the Rhineland now under Allied occupation contrasted markedly with the Algerian trip. In Germany Camus recorded his surprise at finding an atmosphere of normality in an agricultural area spared the heavy bombing that had devastated the country's industrial cities. In a conversation with Camus, an elderly man appealed to 'the eternal peace that Christ brings to all men', an intervention which the perplexed young reporter could only contrast with the crimes of the ss. He ended his piece by evoking 'that wretched Europe, divided between its victims and its executioners (*bourreaux*)' (*CAC*, 560). The pairing of *victimes* and *bourreaux* was to gain prominence in Camus' work and reflected his journalist's appetite for the punchy, schematic formulation of moral dilemmas.

All the while, he was confirming his position as a voice of moral conscience as France emerged from the Second World War. Two days after the atomic bombing of Hiroshima on 6 August 1945, he expressed outrage that the French, American and British press should greet the development as a marvel of scientific achievement. Indignant at what he saw as a 'formidable concert' indecently orchestrated by the media, he offered an alternative verdict: 'mechanical civilization has just reached its final degree of savagery' (*CAC*, 569).

Opposition to the Franco regime was another cause célèbre for Camus and featured in as many as eight of his *Combat* editorials between September 1944 and August 1945. Spain touched a deep chord in him.[7] In an editorial entitled 'Nos frères d'Espagne' (Our Spanish Brothers, 7 September 1944), he wrote of 'this people without equal' (*CAC*, 174). Camus missed no opportunity to argue that the Second World War in Europe had started in Spain in 1936 and he saw as a source of shame the treatment by the French of those fighting against Franco, who were placed under guard when they sought refuge in France. He also rebuked France for failing to foresee in 1938 that what was affecting Spain would spread north. In particular the term 'refugee', he noted, would come to have such 'crushing meaning' (*CAC*, 232) in France in the Second World War. How Spanish refugees came to be treated by the Vichy regime was a further source of dishonour, he reflected, in that they were forced to choose between repatriation to Spain and conscription into units of workers sent to serve the Nazi regime. An impassioned Camus highlighted inconsistencies in the position taken by France towards those fighting dictatorship in Spain and he called for an end to the double standard whereby 'a country . . . exalts the republic and freedom while persecuting those who most proudly defend these values' (*CAC*, 235). He also warned on 24 October 1944 of the continuing risk of a Nazi resurgence facilitated by the Franco regime, an estimated 40,000 Germans, he reported, had fled to Spain and regrouped there in order to exert pressure on the Madrid government).

Insisting on the need for a broad spectrum of anti-Fascist struggle, Camus went on in an editorial of 7–8 January 1945 to criticize Allied moves to establish diplomatic relations with the Franco regime. His invective was intense but he countered the charge that on the issue of Spain he showed excessive passion, urging readers to see that France had to avoid providing respectability to Franco, whom he labelled the accomplice 'of everything that we seek to combat' (*CAC*, 437).

In the months following on from August 1944 when the new *Combat* was launched, Camus' involvement had been intense and he was a daily presence at the paper. But from January 1945, even though he continued to contribute vigorously to the paper, he became gradually more detached.

In his private life the Liberation of Paris meant he could be reunited with his wife and in October 1944 Francine travelled up from Algeria. They lived for a time in a part of André Gide's rue Vaneau flat, which the writer had made available to Camus – Gide himself was in Algiers. With Camus earning a very modest wage at *Combat* and sales of *The Outsider* having been restricted during wartime, he was 'famous but not wealthy'.[8] Food and fuel were also in short supply in the capital and accommodation became a problem for him and Francine when Gide returned to Paris. By the time Camus became a father in September 1945, when Francine gave birth to twins, Catherine and Jean, the family was living outside Paris near Vincennes. They would move back into the city in the following year, securing, in December 1946, a flat in rue Séguier belonging to the Gallimard family.

By that stage *Combat* had started to go into decline. Most of the papers that came out of the Resistance would suffer a similar fate as the momentum of Resistance idealism weakened.[9] With *Combat* facing circulation losses, Camus provided, a year on from his final editorial which had appeared on 15 November 1945, a series of high-profile pieces in November 1946 in an attempt to boost sales.[10] The articles were billed as a reflection on 'The Century of Fear' and grouped under the title 'Ni victimes ni bourreaux' (Neither Victims nor Executioners). Camus described the millions of Europeans who had had their fill of 'violence and lies' (*CAC*, 611) and, with the controversy surrounding the end-of-war purges now behind him, he restated his opposition to any system advocating the death penalty. He reflected that the modern mechanical age had made killing easier by robbing humanity of its knowledge of what execution entailed.

The moral tone of Camus' writing for *Combat* was not to everyone's liking but to those who dismissed his thinking as utopian, he objected that it was a far more dangerous form of utopian thinking that allowed states to legitimize the use of killing. *Sauver les corps* (Save lives, *CAC*, 613) became his watchword and he invited readers to imagine the collapse of state terror which would come with 'the end of ideologies, in other words the collapse of absolute utopias which destroy themselves in history on account of the price they end up exacting' (*CAC*, 621). Camus thus provided an early formulation of the 'end of ideology' mantra which came with the discrediting of Marxism and Fascism in the decades after the Second World War. In the last article in his 'Neither Victims nor Executioners' series – 'Towards Dialogue' (30 November 1946) – he exhorted his readers to hold on to the belief that 'words are stronger than bullets' (*CAC*, 643).[11]

Alongside his new family commitments, his journalism and his work as a professional reader for the publisher Gallimard, Camus was also trying to find room for fiction. The 'Save lives' appeal voiced in the pages of *Combat* was to find an echo in his work on *The Plague*. Camus was now trying to complete the novel, which he presented as part of a new phase in his writing career, the Cycle of Revolt (this to complement the earlier Cycle of the Absurd). His work on *The Plague* stretched back to the war years and was now arousing in him the anxiety that would become increasingly marked in his attempts at literary composition.

Progress on the novel stalled when in March 1946 he went as a guest of the French Cultural Service to North America, where he lectured and travelled. He was away for almost three months. In New York he was greeted by the French *conseiller culturel* (cultural counsellor), the anthropologist Claude Lévi-Strauss. He lectured at Columbia, Vassar College, Wellesley and other East Coast universities and was photographed for *Vogue* by Cecil Beaton. His time in New York also saw the launch of Stuart Gilbert's English translation of *The Outsider* which was brought out by the publisher Alfred Knopf.[12]

On his return to France, Camus set about completing *The Plague*, spending an intense month on it at the home of Michel Gallimard's mother in the Vendée in western France. By September 1946 he was in a position to write to his friend Louis Guilloux to say that he had finished the work, although he expressed grave misgivings about its quality: 'I keep it in my drawer like something that is a bit disgusting.'[13] Replying a few days later, Guilloux acknowledged the effort that such a project required and confided that when he himself had been writing his major novel *Le Sang noir* (translated as *Bitter Victory*), he felt he was literally going to die.[14]

Later that year, Camus posted sections of the work to Saint-Brieuc where Guilloux beavered away making suggestions and corrections. In December, an exchange of telegrams between Camus in Paris and Guilloux in Brittany reflected the frenetic rush to complete the business of reading and checking. Guilloux played down his own role, saying that he had become drawn into commenting on too much of the small detail of the draft novel. But a grateful Camus replied on 27 December, reporting that he had incorporated all of the changes.[15] Camus was keen to stress the theme of a shared pain in *The Plague*, likening the grief of others to that of the narrator, Bernard Rieux: 'it's the secret of the book', he confided to Guilloux. The forthrightly moral language of *Combat* was finding an afterlife in fiction.

Camus ended his letter to Guilloux with the news that he had handed over the typescript that morning to those on the production side at Gallimard. He was relieved to get rid of it: 'Now it's all a haze to me but I am freed from it and it's thanks to you that I have achieved that.'[16] In his inscription of a presentation copy of the novel for Guilloux, Camus would write: '*To Louis Guilloux*, since you wrote this book in part. With the affection of your old brother, A. Camus'.[17]

9

'A Catastrophe Slow to Happen'

The post-war quarrel with Communism was to prove a watershed in Camus' career. On 12 December 1946 he was one of a group of writers and journalists – among them Raymond Queneau, Jean-Bertrand Pontalis, Simone de Beauvoir, Jacques-Laurent Bost and Alexandre Astruc – at a party in the home of Boris and Michelle Vian in the rue du Faubourg-Poissonnière. One of the guests was Maurice Merleau-Ponty, the young philosopher and at that time a Communist sympathizer who had just reviewed Arthur Koestler's *The Yogi and the Commissar* in *Les Temps modernes*, the monthly left-wing journal founded by Sartre after the Second World War.[1]

The Koestler volume had appeared in 1945 and covered issues that Camus was to revisit in *L'Homme révolté* (The Rebel).[2] It was a period of intense ideological debate. For Koestler, himself a former Communist, the Soviet Commissar and the Yogi of his title were polar opposites. The Commissar wanted 'Change from Without' and believed that by transforming the system of economic production and distribution, 'all the pests of humanity' could be eradicated.[3] In sharp contrast, the Yogi rejected all violence, argued that 'the End is unpredictable' and stressed the importance of Means in social change. Whereas the Commissar's sights were trained on Society, the Yogi longed for the Absolute. Koestler issued words of warning to both: to the Soviet Commissar, he quoted Blaise Pascal – 'man is neither angel nor brute, and his misery is that he who would act the angel acts the brute';[4] and he queried the Yogi's position, citing Gandhi's pacifism in the face of Japanese aggression during the Second World War.

In his Koestler review, Merleau-Ponty dismissed the talk of moral purity and the inner life as a form of smokescreen. Moreover, in the alliance between humanism and anti-Communism evoked in Koestler, Merleau-Ponty distinguished between what he saw as a seductive appearance and a less palatable reality, between 'the morality they profess, which is celestial and intransigent, and the morality which they practise which is very much of this world and even hidden'.[5] Concretely in relation to Britain, where Koestler's book had been published, Merleau-Ponty insisted on the discrepancy between the discourse of socialism and democracy and the country's exploitation of its empire.[6] At the core of Merleau-Ponty's critique of Koestler was the former's suspicion about Western humanism and the language of moral intransigence.

This ideological warfare provided the backdrop to the December 1946 gathering at the Vians'. It proved to be a stormy affair. Camus berated Merleau-Ponty, seeing his political position as an implicit acceptance of the trials in the Soviet Union. An ugly scene ensued, with Camus storming out and Sartre and Jacques Bost chasing after him in a vain attempt to persuade him to return. In his diary Camus recorded 'an intolerable loneliness' (OC, II, 1076).

The intense debate about Communism which stretched back to the interwar years was to reach its climax in Camus' case in the row that engulfed *The Rebel* soon after it appeared in 1951. Years later Sartre reflected on the irony of the confrontation that night at Boris Vian's home. He had tried to mediate between two friends on opposing sides politically: 'I was to the right of Merleau, to the left of Camus', he reflected, adding that both writers would later rebuke him for his solidarity with the Communists – Merleau-Ponty resigned from *Les Temps modernes*

Camus campaigning at a rally in the Salle Pleyel in Paris, 3 December 1948, in support of the American activist Garry Davis, self-declared 'citizen of the world'.

in 1953 – and both would die without any reconciliation having taken place (Merleau-Ponty died suddenly in 1961, just over a year after Camus' death in a car crash).[7]

The row or *querelle* with Sartre in 1952 in the wake of the publication of *The Rebel* was to become one of the most high-profile controversies in post-war French culture. The backgrounds of the two adversaries could not have been more different, the accumulated intellectual baggage that came to Sartre from his privileged Schweitzer family connection contrasting with Camus' origins in Belcourt. Sartre had been a brilliant student of philosophy at the Ecole Normale Supérieure in Paris whereas Camus was the cultural outsider, the humorous rascal (the 'petit voyou') from Algiers, as Sartre chose to cast him in a 'Self-portrait' interview to mark his 70th birthday in 1975.

Looking back, Sartre remembered the Camus he met during the war as being great fun, streetwise and someone who did not realize he was a great writer. He recalled that when the four of them were together, Francine Camus and Simone de Beauvoir used to pretend to be shocked by the men's crude language and antics. But Sartre, ever sure of his own worth, added that Camus would quickly take fright when intellectual discussion got complicated.[8] Yet on the Parisian cultural scene in the 1940s, the French Algerian had become a rival to the insider. They were competing on a range of fronts: as novelists, in journalism, philosophy, literary criticism and the theatre; they were the 'two tenors of the French literary scene of their day'.[9] The rivalry could have a bantering tone in the days before the big falling out of 1952. Hence the story told by Simone de Beauvoir of how, on the opening night of Camus' play *Les Justes* (The Just Assassins) on 15 December 1949, a woman admirer rushed up to him after the performance. Not noticing Sartre standing beside him, she remarked how much better his play was than Sartre's *Les Mains sales* (Dirty Hands). Camus, quick as a flash, directed a look of amused complicity in Sartre's direction and replied to the woman with a sardonic smile: 'You're killing two birds with one stone!'[10]

But there was to be no room for banter in the quarrel over *The Rebel*. The virulence of the dispute reflected the ideological tensions in France as the gap between Communist sympathizers and the non-Communist Left emerged in the post-war period. George Orwell's satire *Animal Farm* (1945) formed part of the same ideological debate. In France, where Communists had played a significant role in the Resistance against Fascism, the Communist Party was a force to be reckoned with. There was also a strong awareness in the country of the role played by the Soviet Union in the Allied victory, what the former Communist Edgar Morin referred to as 'the Stalingrad effect'.[11] Not surprisingly much of the literature and journalism of the day reinforced this ideological inflection and to go against this was seen by many as heresy.[12] Revelations about Soviet labour camps, however, saw Camus in 1949 criticize the ambiguous stance of *Les Temps modernes*.[13]

For much of the period when he was writing *The Rebel*, Camus was ill. In the autumn of 1949 he had a relapse of tuberculosis and wrote to his friend the poet René Char, explaining that he had to have bed rest for six weeks followed by months spent living at semi-altitude. He found the withdrawal frustrating. 'I wanted to be *with people*', he stressed.[14]   *The Plague !*

Char congratulated Camus on the success of *Les Justes*, first performed at the Théâtre Hébertot in Paris, with Serge Reggiani and Maria Casares in the lead roles. The play ran for six months. It explored the dilemma facing the revolutionaries of 1905 in Tsarist Russia concerning the issue of violence used as a means to achieve political change. Camus' row with Merleau-Ponty had been precisely about the place of political violence. Merleau's argument was that some forms of political violence had a socially progressive impact, a position which Camus resolutely rejected. Much of this would feed into his reflection in *The Rebel*.

For health reasons, he spent a good part of 1950 at various locations which gave him the altitude that his recovery required. He spent time in Cabris (which sits at a height of over 500 metres in the Alpes-Maritimes), in the Vosges mountains close to the German border and in Savoie. Writing to Char from Cabris in April, he described staying at a hotel on his own with very little human contact, 'not having opened my mouth in a week'.[15] A few weeks later, he wrote that it had been 'a year that is terrible for me in every respect'.[16] In September 1950 he explained to Char that he could not wait to get *The Rebel* finished: 'I imagine stupidly that life will begin afresh then.'[17] He described the painful completion of the manuscript in late February 1951, when, back in Cabris, he confided to Char: 'For the past month, I have been working without interruption. The total solitude and the will to see it through mean that I am spending ten hours a day sitting at the table.' He added inauspiciously that 'the giving birth is long and difficult and it seems to me that the child is indeed ugly. This effort is extenuating.'[18] By 7 March 1951 he had a complete first draft of *The Rebel*.

In his introduction to the essay, Camus made modest claims for the work, seeing it as offering 'merely some historical pointers' and as providing a 'working hypothesis'. It would stand as one attempt among many to analyse the 'démesure' or excess of the age which Camus also labelled 'the prodigious history . . . of European pride' (*oc*, III, 70). Squarely adopting the language of moralism, he asked if human kind was capable of rejecting a State logic of murder which had seen 70 million people killed in half a century. In his advocacy of revolt against the 'privileged position' (*oc*, III, 65) occupied by murder, Camus saw the individual as building community. In a rewriting of Descartes' 'I think, therefore I am', he asserted: 'I revolt, therefore we are' (*oc*, III, 79).

Like Hannah Arendt, who in *The Origins of Totalitarianism* (1951) repudiated both Stalinism and Nazism, Camus proposed a linkage between totalitarian thinking on the Left and on the Right.

eichmann in jerusalem

Left-wing readers of *The Rebel* were affronted by the conflation. Casting Fascism as the expression of 'irrational terror', *The Rebel* explained Stalinism as the creation of a rational terrorism which sought to exterminate the agents of a would-be corrupt order with a view to creating an ideal world. For Camus this amounted to a form of murderous utopianism and he concluded Part III of his essay with a humanist rallying cry: 'Instead of killing and dying to produce the being that we are not, we have to live and have others live to create what we are' (*oc*, III, 277).

In the cultural field, *The Rebel* targeted what its author saw as manifestations of nihilism that were 'freedom-killing' (*oc*, III, 130) in their impact. Camus protested about the gun-running of the poet Arthur Rimbaud in Abyssinia and dismissed Surrealism and its antecedents as expressions of adolescent nihilism. On the subject of *Les Chants de Maldoror* (The Songs of Maldoror) by the nineteenth-century poet the Comte de Lautréamont, he wrote abrasively that the work was nothing other than 'genuine litanies of evil'. It 'exalts "the sanctity of crime"', with stanza twenty of Chant II 'inaugurating . . . a veritable pedagogy of crime and violence' (*oc*, III, 132). Not surprisingly prepublication of some of Camus' material on Lautréamont drew a hostile reception from the prominent Surrealist André Breton.[19] After the full publication of *The Rebel*, Breton commented further on the work (*Arts*, 16 November 1951), Camus responding a couple of days later with a piece entitled 'Révolte et conformisme' (Revolt and Conformism).

Camus was directing his fire against a range of cultural positions. From European political and social history, he picked out the regicides of the French Revolution, Marx's prophecy about a new social order, Stalinist rule in the Soviet Union and the State terror represented by National Socialism. Evoking the killings carried out by Nazis in the obliteration of the Czech village of Lidice in June 1942, he held this up as an example of irrational terror and made a significant link across to European colonial history, saying that similar excesses were committed in the colonies (the English in India in 1857 and the French in Algeria in 1945 – the latter reference being to Sétif and Guelma). These were atrocities committed by 'European nations which in reality obey the same irrational prejudice of racial superiority' (*oc*, III, 219). Camus was thus effectively assembling a loose collage drawn from European political, economic and cultural history.

Release from an invasive History was what he proposed by way of opposition to 'the sound and the fury of the centuries' (*oc*, III, 180). The remedy, he argued, was to be found in revolt, which he defined as the human 'refusal to be treated as an object and to be reduced merely to history' (*oc*, III, 276). In their combative tone Camus' broad-brush formulations reflected the campaigning style of his days at *Combat*.

The ideologically fractured world of post-war culture ensured that *The Rebel* awoke contrasting responses. The right-wing press was sympathetic, Jean Guéhenno in *Le Figaro littéraire* of 24 November 1951 hailing the essay as 'one of the greatest books of the post-war period'. The source of the praise spelled danger for Camus. At the end of December 1951 he wrote in his diary with a sense of foreboding: 'I am patiently awaiting a catastrophe that is slow to happen' (*oc*, IV, 1119).

In the months after the publication of *The Rebel*, there was hesitation at *Les Temps modernes* about who might undertake a review of the work. Eventually the task fell to a young former member of the French Resistance, Francis Jeanson. In a lengthy, hard-hitting account, Jeanson took Camus to task for his attack on History. He also criticized Camus' method of working, complaining about the book's failure to access primary sources when it discussed big-name figures such as Marx. In an interview years later, Jeanson would comment on what he saw as Camus' Mediterranean detachment from the pressing concerns of working-class people living in metropolitan France who were politically committed to the French

Communist Party. Camus was outraged by Jeanson's review and he sent Sartre an indignant reply addressed formally to *Monsieur le Directeur* (The Journal Editor). It was published in *Les Temps modernes* in August 1952.

The same issue of the journal carried a vitriolic response from Sartre. He accused Camus of a 'mixture of gloomy self-importance and vulnerability' which deterred others from being frank with him. Camus had proposed 'Mediterranean measure' (*la pensée de midi*) in *The Rebel* as an antidote to European nihilism but Sartre dismissed such talk as a refusal to engage in debate. He likened reading Camus' letter, which had not been addressed directly to Jeanson, to a viewing of Rembrandt's *The Anatomy Lesson of Dr Nicolaes Tulp*, with a magisterial Camus cast as the doctor and Jeanson as the corpse that is being dissected. Sartre reproached Camus for his overweening sense of indignation: how is it, he wondered, that to criticize Camus is somehow to disenfranchise the poor whom he claims to represent? For the editor of *Les Temps modernes*, the author of *The Rebel* was playing to the gallery, like a lawyer who says of the poor, '"They are my brothers", because those are the words most likely to make members of the jury weep'.[20]

Sartre's text was laced with venom. He dismissed Camus' working-class Algiers origins, insisting that he was now every bit as much a bourgeois as were Jeanson and Sartre. The poverty of his childhood was deemed irrelevant; Sartre accused his rival of pomposity and of an exaggerated, Saint Vincent de Paul-like probity. And what right had Camus, Sartre objected, to exclude Jeanson from the debate with a moral indignation that approximated to a form of racism: '*Who* are you, to assume such distance?'[21]

The assertion that Camus' aloofness would have made him the perfect public prosecutor in 'The Republic of Noble Souls' was not the only slur which Camus would remember when he came to work on *La Chute* (The Fall). Sartre reflected crassly that he hesitated to refer his adversary to his philosophical work *L'Etre et le néant* (Being and Nothingness) because it would be beyond him: 'You cannot abide being intellectually challenged.'[22] There was a self-regarding, almost delirious tone to Sartre's virulence.

Beyond the personal venom, Sartre refuted Camus' claim that *Les Temps modernes* had failed to address the question of the Soviet labour camps. He cited various articles where the situation in the Soviet Union had indeed, he claimed, been discussed. Sartre also protested against bourgeois bad faith in the West, complaining that anti-Communist circles in France had reacted with glee to the discovery of labour camps in Turkmenistan since this provided the ammunition needed to intimidate the defenders of Communism.[23]

Any compliments about Camus' past achievements in Sartre's reply were a calculated move to stress his present isolation. Sartre accepted that his adversary, an outspoken critic of the Franco regime and campaigner against France's colonial politics, had the right to protest about Soviet concentration camps. Indeed he praised Camus' achievements up until 1945, not just his work in the field of literature but his involvement in the Resistance which, Sartre conceded, signalled a strong engagement with History: 'You lived [that contact with History] more deeply and more totally than many of us (including me).'[24] In this role, Camus had, for a number of years, been 'the symbol and the proof of the solidarity between classes'.[25] But to Sartre's dismay, the author of *Letters to a German Friend* had branded the engagement with History a necessary but temporary deviation – Camus reproaches his imaginary German interlocutor for wanting to force him into History. For Sartre, as for Jeanson, the dividing line was clear: in contrast with Camus' wariness, they embraced History as a force that was an inescapable element of human experience. Men were shaped by other men through the workings of class conflict, Sartre argued, and he saw Camus as turning away from this by idealizing the solidarity across classes in the face of death. Sartre concluded sharply that the pressing events of the war had made Camus a figure connected in an intensely vital way with those events; that in 1944 he had embodied the future, but by 1952 he stood for the past.[26]

Looking in on the conflict from the outside, Raymond Aron, a Gaullist *résistant* during the Second World War, philosopher and former *Combat* journalist, chose to stress the similarities rather than the differences between Camus and Sartre. He asked in his *L'Opium des intellectuels* (The Opium of the Intellectuals) why a difference apparently of nuances should have aroused such a conflict, which, he added caustically, would be 'barely comprehensible' outside France and Saint-Germain-des-Prés.[27] 'Neither Sartre nor Camus is a Communist or an "Atlanticist"', Aron reflected, and they could see the iniquities on both sides.[28] Camus was denouncing the Communist East and the capitalist West, Aron went on, whereas Sartre's opprobrium fell on the West even if he did not deny the reality of life in Stalin's Soviet Union. For Aron, neither Sartre nor Camus was a politician – the pen was their route to action and, indeed, however much Sartre opposed the enemies of Communism, the French Communist Party in the early 1950s saw him as an enemy of the people. Aron dryly suggested that in 'Year VII of the Cold War', the two protagonists, were they to have lived behind the Iron Curtain, would both have been liquidated.[29]

Detachment was not something that Camus could easily muster. Back in February 1950 he had expressed the hope that once he had finished *The Rebel*, he would have 'the freedom to be and to express'.[30] The mauling the work had received in *Les Temps modernes* put paid to that. There was support from some leading thinkers, including Hannah Arendt and Paul Ricoeur. The theologians Etienne Gilson and Père Henri de Lubac also gave *The Rebel* their backing. But the quarrel with Sartre and *Les Temps modernes* was to cloud and in many ways shape the rest of Camus' professional life. It had been a bruising affair and he confided to his wife Francine that he was 'paying a heavy price for this wretched book'.[31]

It meant intense public humiliation for him. Other journals had also carried attacks on *The Rebel* – *Arts*, where André Breton lodged his protest as we have seen, the right-wing weekly *Carrefour* and the far-right *Rivarol*. The whole episode left Camus warier than ever about life in Saint-Germain-des-Prés: 'September [19]52. . . . Paris is a jungle and its wild cats are seedy-looking', he wrote in his diary (*OC*, IV, 1146). As Maria Casares confided to the Mexican poet Octavio Paz, Camus paced up and down in private 'like a wounded bull'.[32] In a letter of 9 August 1952 sent from Le Panelier to Louis Guilloux, he wrote of his devastation: *Je suis dans le noir total* (I am in utter despair).[33]

10

Wars of Words Continued

Since their first meeting in the summer of 1945 in the Gallimard premises in Paris, a strong affinity had existed between Guilloux and Camus. In December of that year, Camus wrote to the author from Saint-Brieuc to say that he had 'a hundred reasons to feel close to you and I hope that life will allow me to prove this to you'.[1] They came from similar social backgrounds. Both were committed to the working class and both had started out as members of the Communist Party before becoming disillusioned. Dedicating a copy of *The Rebel* to Guilloux, Camus singled him out as 'one of the few to know what the book represents for me'.[2]

Back in September 1939, while working for *Alger républicain*, he had begun serializing Guilloux's *La Maison du peuple* (The House of the People). It was a work he had admired ever since Jean Grenier got him to read it back in the Grand Lycée in Algiers. But the censors quickly intervened, as we have seen, banning a novel which depicted proletarian militancy. After the war Camus was again keen to promote Guilloux's work and indeed to help make more secure its author's financial position. The journalist Jean Daniel, who would go on to launch *Le Nouvel Observateur*, recalls how as the young editor of the review *Caliban*, he received a call from Camus out of the blue. Camus was 'a God for my generation', he reflected.[3] Asked what he had lined up for future numbers of the review, Daniel sheepishly explained that for the following month it was to be a republication of Tolstoy's *The Death of Ivan Ilyich*. With Daniel then hesitating, Camus asked if he might make a suggestion: *La Maison du peuple* by Louis Guilloux. A flattered Daniel accepted straight away and in January 1948 *Caliban* republished a work which had first appeared back in 1927.

La Maison du peuple now came with a preface by Camus, who praised Guilloux's understated narrative of working-class poverty. The work showed, Camus noted, an insider's knowledge of the world of hardship. Like his contemporary Eugène Dabit and the nineteenth-century novelist Jules Vallès, Guilloux neither flattered nor despised 'the people', Camus enthused. As Jean Daniel commented years later, the fit between the Guilloux and *Caliban* was perfect in a journal whose Shakespearean title – with its connotation of social exclusion – was intended to signal the connection between the people and literature.[4]

Camus commended Guilloux for avoiding sentimentalism and facile realism and for achieving a tone reminiscent of Tolstoy's novellas. His greatest achievement in Camus' view was his capacity to lay bare the other's pain, to be 'the novelist of suffering' who allowed his protagonists to acquire a universal appeal while having them experience 'the most humble reality'.[5] In *La Maison du peuple*, living with poverty is depicted as deadening. On low wages and toiling in a workshop, Camus concludes, Tristan no longer has anything to say to Isolde.

Yet his endorsement of Guilloux also carried an element of calculated provocation. All too often in France, he complained, the world of poverty was described by bourgeois authors with no experience of the condition. In rejecting the 'periodicals and books drawn up by the specialists in progress' (*oc*, II, 712) who describe the working class, Camus objected, as though it were an exotic tribe, he preferred to heed those who had direct experience of the condition. Or, as he put it, he would settle for the testimony of those who told their tale after having the knife put to their throats, so to speak (*oc*, II, 711–12). Camus was thus laying claim to a particular view of proletarian life experience and seeking to counter the Marxist belief in a workers' march towards self-realization. Guilloux, he stressed, showed poverty isolating individuals rather than drawing them into community. In that isolation, Camus found a mirroring of his own social representation in *The Wrong Side and the Right Side*. In the short story 'The Silent Ones' in the collection *Exile and the Kingdom*, Camus evokes the life of factory workers who feel marginalized, their manual skills now redundant, 'their rough, useless hands hanging down by their old trousers covered with sawdust' (*EK*, 40).

Camus' preface to the 1948 Guilloux publication again featured in the Grasset edition of the novel, which came out in 1953, the year after the very public quarrel with Sartre. This new context ensured that the preface did not go unnoticed. Claude Roy, writing on 28 October in *Libération*, a paper supported by the French Communist Party, took Camus to task for arguing that it was only those who had experienced poverty who were qualified to write about it. Dismissing the preface to Guilloux's novel as a 'little masterpiece of demagoguery', Roy countered that poverty was as offensive to those who came across it as it was to those who were in it. Tolstoy, La Bruyère, Turgenev and Pirandello were all held up by Roy for their commitment to such representation.[6]

The Cold War context again provided the driver. From Jean Daniel, Guilloux learnt that *Libération* was actively targeting Camus, who in June 1953 had been prominent at a meeting held in the Salle de la Mutualité in Paris to protest about the shooting of German workers in East Berlin by Soviet troops.[7] *Libération* went on to publish on 12 November 1953 a letter of complaint by Guilloux, together with Claude Roy's reply. Guilloux suggested that Roy had heaped praise on *La Maison du peuple* in order to denigrate Camus. Roy objected that being born into the working class was no guarantee of talent and that what needed to be asked of bourgeois like Marx, Engels, Sartre and Louis Aragon was whether or not their analyses were well founded.

Roy went on to remind readers of a situation faced by Camus himself in July that year. Camus had written to *Le Monde* to protest against the killing of seven North African demonstrators in Paris's Place de la Nation on Bastille Day. He suggested in his letter that the dead were victims of a conspiracy of silence involving many newspapers and parliamentarians. It was, wrote Camus, 'a racism that dared not speak its name' (*oc*, III, 908). Yet as Roy pointed out, Camus came to be vilified by colonialists who objected that as a European, he had no right to be speaking out in favour of 'Arabs'. For Roy, Camus' views on the subject of who was best placed to speak about the poor risked falling into a similarly reactionary typecasting.[8]

Spain was another piece in the Cold War jigsaw, Camus arguing vociferously that the dictatorship there represented unfinished business from the Second World War. At *Combat* he had been out-spoken about Franco's rule and in a speech made at the Salle Wagram on 30 November 1952, 'L'Espagne et la culture' (Spain and Culture), he protested against the country's recent admission to UNESCO. For him it represented a further step in the rehabilitation of a regime seeking to acquire the moral respectability that allowed it to function. The day was coming, he complained, when 'a hand-ful of military commanders and industrialists' (*oc*, III, 435) would lay claim to Molière and Voltaire. Why, he asked, should the Spain of Franco be admitted to an organization whose mission was to develop cultural and educational links when the real cultural tradition in Spain, that of Cervantes and Unamuno, had been dishonoured and when the work of a poet who was a victim of nationalist violence, Federico García Lorca, was now subject to state censorship. With Spain joining UNESCO, Camus reflected sarcastically that, had Hitler and Mussolini been alive, they too might have aspired to hold positions there.

Camus rehearsed and then refuted the reasons for Western support for Spain: first, the imperative of respecting the principle of non-intervention in the affairs of a nation state; and second, the status of Fascist Spain as a bulwark against Communism in the Cold War. Camus' point was that the continuation of a Fascist regime served as ammunition to those promoting Communism. In the Europe of the early 1950s, he concluded, 'the maintenance of a totalitarian regime means sooner or later the strengthening of Communism' (*oc*, iii, 437).

For Camus, anti-Semitism, Fascism, the concentration camps and the show trials in the Soviet Union all constituted a testing ground for 'the sincerity of democratic politics' (*oc*, iii, 437). Governments which supported Franco diminished themselves, he argued, adding that the respectability achieved by the Spanish government was nothing more than a 'consolidation of crime'. He appealed to all those, Spanish and non-Spanish alike, 'who reject crime from wherever it comes' (*oc*, iii, 438).

Summing up for his Salle Wagram audience in November 1952, Camus reflected that what united them was their will to protest against 'a haggling which hides behind the screen of culture' (*oc*, iii, 438). He was a tenacious advocate, as his combative, tightly woven formulations make clear: 'cultural associations come and go but culture remains', he reassured his audience, adding that 'true culture lives on truth and dies from lies' – in the original French his use of alliteration added to the polemical charge: 'La *v*raie culture *v*it de *v*érité et *m*eurt de *m*ensonge' (*oc*, iii, 439).

In a final rallying cry, Camus insisted that culture's seedbed lay far from the carceral regime of Madrid and from the plush buildings of unesco. He argued that it was into the space of freedom, the space of writers and free men, that Spain would be welcomed by those who recognized in that country's traditions and culture the source of 'our greatest lessons' (*oc*, iii, 439). When Spain secured admission to the United Nations in 1955, he was to be no less outspoken.[9]

As a public figure, then, Camus did not shy away from taking a position – the quarrel with Sartre, opposing dictatorship in Spain, intervening in favour of workers' rights in East Berlin, speaking out about the treatment of North African protestors in Paris. On the big issues of the Cold War, colonialism and the condition of the working class, he was engaged and interventionist.

Among the authors promoted by Camus in the book series Espoir (Hope), which he directed for Gallimard, Simone Weil's work, published posthumously, was especially prominent. Weil's *La Condition ouvrière* (The Condition of the Working Class, 1951) charts her experience when she left teaching to begin work in a Renault factory in Saint-Etienne in late 1934. She came from a privileged bourgeois background. Yet in his brief preface to her essay, Camus writes pointedly that it was not the work of an intellectual desperate to live 'extreme experiences' (*OC*, III, 886). In other words, in Camus' eyes Weil was not playing at being proletarian.

These ideological tensions were feeding through into his fiction. In the short story 'The Silent Ones', the factory worker Yvars re-inforces Camus' message about talkers and doers: feeling the physical strain, the worker complains that 'those who made big speeches about manual work did not know what they were talking about' (*EK*, 39). The suspicion directed against the bourgeois intellectual was to be a recurring position in Camus' career. In the Paris of the 1950s it meant pronounced isolation for him, a situation that would be reflected in his wariness as a writer who nevertheless remained very much in the public eye.

11

Beyond Polemic: 'From Now On, Creation'

The illusions I create with my painting are what is most real in me. The rest is moving sand.

Eugène Delacroix[1]

Sometime before the dramatic row with Sartre over *The Rebel* that so undermined Camus, he had already recorded his sense of disillusionment with professional life in Paris. The philosopher Paul Ricœur was to observe that, seen from the provinces, the Paris of Saint-Germain-des-Prés seemed 'like a superficial fable'.[2] Camus' verdict was couched in a different language. In a diary entry for the summer of 1951, he reflected that the Gallimard publishing house was an 'odd milieu which is supposed to bring writers on and where nevertheless one loses the joy of writing and creating' (*oc*, IV, 1106). There was a strong libertarian streak in Camus and he recoiled from institutionalization: 'I have never been very submissive in my attitude to the world and to prevailing opinions' (*oc*, IV, 1120), he recorded shortly afterwards in his diary.

His isolation in this period was mirrored in the subjects on which he chose to work. In November 1952 he published a brief entry on Herman Melville for the series Ecrivains célèbres (Famous Writers).[3] Camus was a huge admirer of Melville. He stressed the isolation in which the American novelist found himself when, after success as a writer in the 1840s, his *Moby-Dick; or, the Whale* (1851) received a hostile reception. Melville the artist, he wrote, was forced into a spell of 'total silence', undertaking clerical work in the Port of New York. The identification of the beleaguered Camus with his predecessor was clear from his presentation of Melville's life during the decade 1856–66 which Camus simplified in order to heighten the image of a writer destroyed by his critics.[4]

Camus was feeling acutely the isolation and estrangement that had come with his experience as a high-profile writer. He had noted in his diary in 1951 how when listening to some recordings that he had made for radio, he felt exasperated by a stiffness of tone in the voice born of wariness. 'Paris makes me this way, however much I try', he noted (*oc*, IV, 1119). Too much time spent alone, he feared, lay behind this. Gone were the old days at *Combat* where interaction with others had been life-giving.

He felt the same nostalgia for the collective work of the theatre, remembering his experience as a member of the Théâtre de l'Equipe back in Algiers in the mid-1930s. In June 1953 he threw himself into the Festival at Angers. His modern French version of Pierre de Larivey's comedy *Les Esprits* was performed, the figure of the miser providing the subject of the play (Larivey had adapted the figure from Lorenzino de' Medici and Molière's *L'Avare* (The Miser) would later pick up on the same subject). Also performed at the Festival was Camus' French rendering of *La Devoción de la cruz* (The Devotion to the Cross), a play by the Spanish Golden Age dramatist Calderón de la Barca which Marcel Herrand had directed (Herrand died just before the festival opened). The performance of the Calderón against the backdrop of the chateau of Angers was a big success and Camus felt lifted.[5]

Working out precisely what the role of the artist should be was a pressing question for him. He concluded his 'current reflections' for the years 1948–53, *Actuelles II*, with a mock interview entitled 'The Artist and His Times' in which he explained that as an artist he had not been so pretentious as to cast himself primarily in the role of witness. Camus disliked being presented as the moral conscience of his day. As a human being, he insisted, happiness was what interested him and as an artist he still had work to do – 'characters to bring to life without the help of wars and courtrooms' (oc, iii, 451). Yet the events of his day had, in his words, sought him out as much as everyone else.

Defending the artist's autonomy was his riposte to the hammering given to *The Rebel* in *Les Temps modernes*. He dismissed the claims of Marxism, seeing in the belief in a future, classless society a Romantic pretention that was fundamentally religious and involved no less mystification than the process whereby colonialist oppression was dressed up as the need to save the souls of the infidels (oc, iii, 452). Artists may not feel the need to intervene in the events of their century, Camus insisted, yet as human beings they do; he cited the cases of mine workers, the 'slaves of the camps' (a reference to the Soviet Union) and the 'slaves of the colonies' (oc, iii, 453).

Camus suggested that from his earliest work, he had expressed solidarity with 'those who are humiliated and downtrodden' (oc, iii, 454). For him, the values to be found in the lone writer's creation and those of humanity were therefore not mutually exclusive and he offered as examples of the successful holding in equilibrium of such values the works of Molière, Tolstoy and Melville. The artists of his day, he went on, might be retreating into the isolation of the ivory tower or joining 'the social church'. But both temptations had to be resisted: a 'long patience' on the part of the artist would ensure that art remained 'the enemy of no-one' while encapsulating an expression of social freedom (oc, iii, 454–5).

Public controversy had sapped Camus' energy. In his diary, he noted: 'October 1953: Publication of *Actuelles ii*. The inventory is complete – commentary and polemic. From now on, creation' (oc, iv, 1179).[6] Yet the return to art, however much he craved it, proved difficult. In the autumn of 1953, his wife Francine fell into a state of depression which was to last for the best part of a year. It was a period of disarray for Camus and for part of it he felt unable to write. Indeed his literary output in terms of actual publications in the years after *The Rebel* was to remain slim.

Gradually he set about working into literature some of what life had thrown at him in the crisis years of the early 1950s. The six short stories that were to make up *Exile and the Kingdom* in 1957 carried the dedication 'To Francine'. They provide a series of tense narratives in which the subject of exile, both literal and metaphorical, is explored. One of the narratives where the biographical echoes are strong, 'Jonas ou l'Artiste au travail' (Jonas; or, The Artist at Work), tells the story of a painter living in Paris whose experience of artistic success has been deeply alienating. A friend, Rateau, remarks about the artist's admirers: 'They want you to stand still, like a statue . . . you're not allowed to live' (*EK*, 67). For Camus' artist, typecast and diminished by fame, his plight derives from his inability to reconcile his art and life. Jonas reflects on the psychological distress caused to his wife by his loss of creativity, his womanizing and his retreat into isolation. Her plight allows the artist to see that he has no monopoly on the experience of desperation: 'how deeply the wear and tear of their life had affected her too' (*EK*, 78). As the story reaches its conclusion, an exhausted Jonas, resolving no longer to paint, feels the relief of reconnection with those around him and glimpses the prospect of a new beginning, a *vita nuova*.

Abandoning writing altogether was something Camus seriously entertained in the 1950s. In August 1957, a few months after publication of *Exile and the Kingdom*, he would record in his diary during a stay in Cordes in the Tarn region: 'overwhelming doubt about my vocation. I am seriously considering the possibility of giving up' (*OC*, IV, 1261). This was no empty rhetoric. Doubtless thinking of the imminent return to Paris, he asked dejectedly who it was that writers wrote for, observing that literary circles were places of meanness and mediocrity and that in bourgeois society more

A 1950s shot of the marketplace in Ghardaïa in the Algerian desert, by Swiss photographer Henriette Grindat. Grindat also worked with Camus and René Char in a text-and-photographic-image collaboration which led to the publication of *La Postérité du soleil* (The Posterity of the Sun).

generally, people might read no more than two books a year, books that happened to be in fashion. He complained of making 'this incessant effort which makes me unhappy' and wondered if working in the theatre might be the solution. Others greater than him, he added, had renounced writing.

In his preparatory work for the *Exile and the Kingdom* narratives, Camus had worked Algeria into a prominent position. On a trip there in December 1952 he had visited Oran and Algiers and also travelled alone inland by car, visiting Laghouat and, further south, Ghardaïa in the Mzab region. The visit saw him sketch out plans for the individual stories in the collection. In February 1954 Editions de l'Empire in Algiers published one of them in illustrated form, *La Femme adultère* (The Adulterous Wife). The story of Camus' heroine Janine reprises the question of the European's place in Algeria. On a visit to the southern territories, she becomes acutely aware of her separateness from the indigenous people and the landscape. The infidelity suggested by the story's title derives from her would-be transgressive longing for connection with what is native.

If Camus was exercised by the subject of 'The Artist and His Times', that preoccupation was set to deepen with the course of events in Algeria. November 1954 saw the beginning of what was to develop into the Algerian War of Independence and on 31 March 1955 the French declared a state of emergency there. Camus dramatizes the place of the European settler in *Exile and the Kingdom* in the story 'L'Hôte', an ambiguous title since the term denotes both a guest and a host. The narrative explores the question: whose home is Algeria? Three male figures are juxtaposed in the story: the European Algerian policeman Balducci, who speaks in racist terms of the Algerian Muslim prisoner accused of homicide and hands him over to Daru, the French Algerian schoolteacher living a spartan existence in the outback and tending to the needs of his Muslim pupils at a time of famine. With his role idealized by Camus, Daru is cast as the good European. He offers hospitality to the Arab prisoner, albeit reluctantly, before himself becoming a victim: he receives a death threat from local Arabs who wrongly assume that he has handed their brother over to colonial justice. In the resonance chamber of fiction with its Daru/Camus echo, the fears of the liberal-minded French Algerian in the 1950s are given free expression.

Violence in North Africa is again the focus in another of the stories in *Exile and the Kingdom* – 'Le Renégat' (The Renegade).

This melodramatic narrative involving a European missionary and his contact with a pagan African tribe provides a deranged reflection on interethnic violence and mutilation. Camus first published the narrative in the *Nouvelle Revue française* in June 1956 under the title 'Un esprit confus' (A Confused Mind). Given the inescapable backdrop of the Algerian War and the story's intense depiction of violence as a form of engulfment, the link between literature and life could not have been more pressing.[7]

Camus concluded *Exile and the Kingdom* with a story he had started working on back in the summer of 1949 during a trip to South America. 'La Pierre qui pousse' (The Growing Stone) is set in the Brazilian rainforest. Tellingly it is in this location that the European protagonist D'Arrast finds a welcome within the indigenous community. Camus idealizes the exotic setting of an equatorial rainforest in which the European outsider is invited by local tribespeople to occupy the place made vacant for him and thus to commune with them: the invitation '"Sit down with us"' (*EK*, 109) closes the narrative. Memory of the rainforest was providing what a polarized, violent Algeria could no longer deliver.

In his early work Camus had made much of the allure of the Mediterranean, stressing the influence of ancient Greece in the shaping of that culture. A trip to Greece in late April–May 1955 saw him rekindle that enthusiasm. He lectured at the French Institute in Athens on the subject of 'The Future of Tragedy', before going on as a tourist to visit Delphi, the Peloponnese and the island of Delos.

In his notebooks, Camus wrote exuberantly about his stay, recording details of his surroundings with the eye of a landscape gardener. He enthused about the teamwork of a group of archaeologists working on the ruins of Argos. One of them, Georges Roux, a young man from the Vaucluse, Camus described as being 'so vivacious, so passionate about his beautiful profession' (*OC*, IV, 1225). The writer felt envious, the emotion causing him to think of the wasted time of recent years and of 'my profound feeling of weakness'.

Camus at a book signing in the mid-1950s. His own work *Actuelles* is on display as is Albert Memmi's *La Statue de sel* (Pillar of Salt), first published in 1953. Camus then wrote a preface for the American translation of Memmi's novel which came out in 1955.

The spectacle of the archaeologists happily collaborating prompted him to write on 2 May 1955:

I have only ever been happy and at peace when engaged in a . . . task accomplished with other men whom I can love. I don't have a *métier* [craft, profession], only a vocation. And my work is solitary. I must accept that . . . But I cannot avoid a sense of melancholy when I find myself with those who are happy with what they are doing (*oc*, IV, 1226).

At the end of the trip to Greece on 15 May 1955, Camus savoured the last hours spent on the sea off Athens: 'they are for me hours of farewell to this country which for weeks has poured out to us the same long joy' (*oc*, IV, 1234).

By then, Camus had agreed to write for the liberal paper *L'Express* and he filed his first report from Greece, covering an earthquake in the port city of Volos. Political considerations had influenced his return to journalism. He supported Pierre Mendès-France, who had shown himself to be a reformist minister in the area of colonial politics, bringing an end to France's war in Indochina and seeking to end French rule in Tunisia. Camus saw his own contribution at *L'Express* as a way of providing backing for Mendès' progressivism.

Two articles on Algeria published on 9 and 23 July 1955 saw Camus calling for colonization to be replaced by an association between the Algerian and European Algerian populations and for 'a common liberation' for 'French and Arabs' (*oc*, III, 1033). On 20 August that year, supporters of the FLN, the National Liberation Front, killed and mutilated Europeans and Muslims opposed to the FLN in the Philippeville region (today Skikda). This led to violent repression by the French army and by French Algerian vigilante groups, with thousands of deaths. The pattern of Sétif in May 1945 thus came to be repeated, Philippeville marking the beginning of what François Mitterrand, France's Minister of the Interior when the Algerian War broke out in November 1954, would later refer to as the country's 'infernal circle' of insurrection and repression.[8]

Camus continued to set out his position on Algeria in a series of articles for *L'Express* written between 18 October 1955 and 2 February 1956, arguing that 'Algeria is not France' but reminding his metropolitan readers that the country's population included a million French.[9] He was no less forthright in defending the rights of Algerian immigrant workers in France against a hostile press and a racist police force (*oc*, III, 1052). In the same article on the subject of 'the law of contempt' (29 November 1955), he described as 'idiotic' the clichéd view in France that all French Algerians were colonialists and that all Arabs living in Paris were organizers of prostitution.

Back in the autumn of 1953, Camus had written that, unlike a night of excess, there was no easy remedy for history's hangovers (*oc*, IV, 1179). The situation in Algeria was proof of that. In the wake of Philippeville, the conflict intensified and it was raised at the General Assembly of the United Nations that autumn. In March 1956 the French government enacted special powers for its pursuit of the conflict, which in France remained *la guerre sans nom* (the war without a name).

Camus himself attempted a very public intervention in Algeria in January 1956, campaigning for a truce that would protect the country's civilian population from the effects of the war being waged between the French army and the FLN. On 10 January 1956 in *L'Express*, after noting an increase in reports received of atrocities in Algeria, Camus suggested that 'Algeria will soon be inhabited only by murderers and victims. Soon only the dead there will be innocent' (*oc*, IV, 367). Arguing that 'the long colonialist violence explained the violence of the rebellion', he urged French Algerians not to make, as he put it, the suicidal move of supporting the right-wing Poujadists but rather to work to understand what motivated Algerian nationalists. He proposed a different political language: in order to establish 'a loyal collaboration between the different sons of a common land', he called for a civilian truce (*oc*, IV, 369).

Once back in Algiers, Camus discovered that the anxiety which he had been experiencing in Paris had now left him. In a diary entry for 18 January 1956, he noted that

here at least one is where the struggle is, a hard one for us since public opinion is against us. But it's in the struggle that I have always ended up finding my peace. The professional intellectual

Camus and typesetter Georges Roy at the newspaper *L'Express* in the mid-1950s.
They had also worked together on *Combat* a decade earlier.

... especially if his only involvement in public affairs is via the
written word lives like a coward ... It's only when thought
entails risk that it comes to be justified. And then too, anything
is better than the France of nastiness, the France that abdicates
its responsibilities. That's the swamp in which I am suffocating
(*oc*, IV, 1241).

But having lived away from Algeria for a number of years, Camus
had work to do to understand the new situation. At a tense meeting held in the Cercle du Progrès on Place du Gouvernement on 22
January (the right-wing mayor of Algiers had refused the organizers
access to the Hôtel de Ville), Camus anxiously made his 'Appel à
une trêve civile' (Appeal for a Civilian Truce). Outside the building,
French Algerian loyalists had gathered and were calling for Camus
to be strung up. Among those present at the meeting were liberal-
minded French Algerians including Jean de Maisonseul, moderate
Muslims and also figures such as Amar Ouzegane and Mohamed

Lebjaoui, who were later to assume prominent roles in the FLN. Lebjaoui later described Camus' tense, anxious demeanour as he addressed his audience.[10] The truce initiative failed and Camus felt he had been used by the FLN – unbeknown to him, Lebjaoui, Ouzegane and others were already associated with the Liberation Movement.[11] Three years later, he would testify on behalf of Ouzegane, then on trial for his part in the uprising. Camus cited Ouzegane's positive role in the search for a civilian truce.[12]

On his January 1956 trip Camus also met Jacques Soustelle, the governor general of Algeria, who was unconvinced that the call for a truce would work. Ferhat Abbas, then a moderate Algerian nationalist, had been present at the meeting and soon afterwards would join forces with the FLN. The gap between France and the French Algerians came sharply into focus on 6 February 1956 when the newly appointed head of state Guy Mollet was pelted with tomatoes in Algiers by a hostile French Algerian crowd intent on frustrating any moves to liberalize French rule in the colony. There were other signs of what for Camus was a disturbing drift. He disagreed with the owner and editor of *L'Express* Jean-Jacques Servan-Schreiber, whose line on Algeria was not to rule out any solution to the conflict, including independence.[13] Camus resigned from *L'Express*, his last article for the paper appearing on 2 February 1956. It was 'Remerciement à Mozart' (In Gratitude to Mozart), marking the bicentenary of the composer's birth. The choice of subject told its own story, for it signalled a turning away from public pronouncement on a conflict in which Camus was to feel increasingly marginalized.

12

Staging Confession

On a trip to Amsterdam back in October 1954, Camus had started taking notes for *La Chute* (The Fall), which at the outset he saw as a short story for inclusion in *Exile and the Kingdom*. The story drew its energy from the recrimination that had surrounded the reception of *The Rebel*. Memories of Sartre's diatribe at the height of the affair in the summer of 1952 were rekindled for Camus when, on 6 December 1954, Simone de Beauvoir was awarded the Goncourt Prize for *Les Mandarins* (The Mandarins). Beauvoir's novel carried a barely disguised, unflattering portrait of Camus in the role of the newspaper editor Henri Perron. Camus was on a lecture tour in Italy when the Goncourt news was announced. But a diary entry at the end of that trip gave a flavour of what he was coming back to mentally in Paris: '*14 December. Departure.* Existentialism. When they accuse themselves, one can be sure that it is always to enable them to accuse others. Judge-penitents.'[1]

The protagonist in *The Fall*, Jean-Baptiste Clamence, was to be one such 'judge-penitent'. A former Parisian lawyer who presides in a seedy bar in Amsterdam, he dispenses justice in accordance with a structured, oppressive routine: having catalogued his own moral failings (as penitent), he proceeds remorselessly to pass judgement on his interlocutor. In Clamence's world, guilt inexorably becomes the condition of the age.

In the blurb for the Espoir series which he directed at Gallimard, Camus had attempted to capture the post-war zeitgeist: 'We live in an age of nihilism. Can we get out of nihilism?' he asked, urging his readers to 'find the cure at the end of the disease' and to recognize that 'it is the time of hope, even if it is a difficult hope.' This hand-on-heart rallying cry to a generation emerging from the war throws into relief the world of edgy masquerade which Camus deftly constructed in *The Fall*. There Clamence, with his 'disdainful confession' as Maurice Blanchot termed it, aspires to bring about a collective descent into nihilistic recrimination and guilt.[2] He describes himself as a latter-day John the Baptist wandering in a modern urban desert. But unlike his New Testament predecessor, he is an 'empty prophet for a time of mediocrity, Elijah without a Messiah' (*oc*, III, 751). In a letter to Alfred Rosmer, Camus explained what lay behind *The Fall*: 'Guilt is something I share and yet it does not subjugate me. But elsewhere it is having that effect. And this explains the incomprehensible phenomenon of the cultivated Westerner approving of what is worst . . . From now on, the solution is clear: we need to heal that guilt, heal that Christianity without God.'[3]

In *Les Temps modernes* in 1952, Sartre had mocked Camus, casting him as a public prosecutor in 'The Republic of Noble Souls'.[4] He had accused him of sulking and of threatening to run off to the desert, of sounding like an investigating magistrate: 'I thought I was dealing with a writer and I am dealing with a judge', Sartre had complained.[5]

Camus' manoeuvre in the pages of *The Fall* was to disarm his adversary by appearing to absorb avidly the strands of Sartre's diatribe, with talk of deserts, judgements and forensic examination all finding their way into Clamence's uninterrupted monologue. By discrediting his protagonist's discursive posturing, Camus was in a sense throwing back with biting irony the many charges Sartre had laid at his door – the affectation of probity, the pose of siding with the weak and the poor, the promotion of himself as the moral conscience of his age.

Camus' choice of genre for *The Fall* was also unexpected. As he explained in his last interview in December 1959, 'in that work I used a theatrical technique (dramatic monologue and implicit dialogue)' (*oc*, IV, 663). If his ability to sustain creative writing had been seriously compromised by the loss of confidence in the wake of the row with Sartre, the play-in-prose format of *The Fall* was the terrain, the stage of ambiguity on which a still bruised Camus now chose to fight back. The work expanded, outgrowing the format that would have allowed for its inclusion in *Exile and the Kingdom*, and it was published as a separate volume by Gallimard in May 1956.

If Camus was halfway into theatre in the pages of *The Fall*, the stage work proper that he took on in the 1950s again shows him working with narratives of confession, albeit more authentic confession than the one paraded by Clamence. For the Angers Festival in June 1953, he translated Calderón's *The Devotion to the Cross*, in which the villainous Eusebio seeks divine mercy and miraculously finds it in the play's melodramatic finale through his devotion to the cross. In a foreword to the translation, Camus spoke of his attempt to make the play sound contemporary. He particularly wanted to draw into a modern context the notion of 'grace that transforms the worst criminals' and he suggested a link between Calderón and the 'All is grace' conclusion to *Journal d'un curé de campagne* (The Diary of a Country Priest) by Georges Bernanos, a novelist whose work Camus greatly admired: 'the "All is grace" . . . attempts to respond in the modern conscience to the "Nothing is just" of the unbelievers' (*oc*, III, 515). All the while, Camus was wrestling with questions to do with ethical value and continuing to address the quandary he posed in the blurb for Gallimard's Espoir series: 'Can we get out of nihilism?'

Adapting and staging William Faulkner's *Requiem for a Nun* allowed Camus to extend this work on the motifs of confession and punishment. It was to be his first time directing a play in Paris and his reworking of Faulkner's narrative of expiation from the American South was to prove a big success.

Requiem for a Nun appeared originally as a dialogue novel in America in 1951. Twenty years earlier Malraux had brought Faulkner to the attention of an enthusiastic French reading public. For Malraux, Sanctuary (1931) contained elements of Greek tragedy. In his promotion of Requiem for a Nun, Camus hailed Faulkner as the greatest writer of his day and placed his work alongside that of Melville, Dostoyevsky and Proust. Marcel Herrand had planned to adapt the novel for the stage and when he died in June 1953 Camus was keen to take the project forward. A fair amount of

The Gallimard front cover for Camus' adaptation of William Faulkner's Requiem for a Nun (1956).

time was spent securing authorization for the adaptation, after which Camus pressed ahead, with rehearsals beginning on 10 August 1956.[6]

There was much anticipation in the run-up to the first night. Faulkner had received the Nobel Prize for Literature back in 1950 and a headline in *Le Monde* on 31 August 1956 asked if this collaboration between two major writers might deliver 'a first modern tragedy' (*oc*, III, 845). In the initial contacts between America and France on the question of permissions, the role of Ruth Ford – who had adapted Faulkner's novel for the stage, stripping out the prose sections and focusing on the three acts – was overlooked. The result was that Camus based his text for the performance on Ford's adapted version while believing this to be Faulkner's own adaptation.[7] Louis Guilloux's translation from the English provided a base text to which others subsequently contributed. Camus himself made some modifications, steering away for example from the emphasis placed on the religious dimension of expiation late in Faulkner's original version.

Camus had been scouring the Paris theatres as he worked to put together his cast. He recruited the French Algerian actress Catherine Sellers for the role of Temple Drake, the young American mother whose past in the world of prostitution returns to haunt her. Tatiana Moukhine, an Egyptian-born actress of Russian origin, appeared in the role of Nancy Mannigoe, the black servant who kills Temple's infant child in order to prevent it becoming a victim of the sordid world that Temple appears on the verge of rejoining and which Nancy herself had known. After 70 rehearsals, including four full dress rehearsals, *Requiem pour une nonne* opened on 20 September 1956 at the Théâtre des Mathurins-Marcel Herrand.[8] It proved to be a huge success, enjoying an unbroken run on the Paris stage until January 1958. René Char wrote immediately to Camus to congratulate him. In his reply, Camus said how surprised he and the actors were and recorded the enjoyment he had experienced as director of the play: 'It's a beautiful and mysterious craft', he enthused.[9] The press hailed the work as a triumph, with Jean-Jacques Gautier in *Le Figaro* commending the cast, especially Catherine Sellers, 'a young and authentic tragedian'.[10]

When news came through of Camus' Nobel Prize in October 1957, the Théâtre des Mathurins could boast in its autumn programme notes that it had 'the rare honour of having two winners of the Nobel Prize for Literature on the same bill'. After its Paris run, the play went on tour to Switzerland, Germany, Belgium, Luxembourg and North Africa. When it was performed in Athens in March 1957, Faulkner himself was present. It was Camus' greatest success in the theatre. In September 1961, the year after his death, the play would again be staged in Paris, with Catherine Sellers and Tatiana Moukhine reappearing at the Théâtre des Mathurins in their original roles and again to public acclaim.[11]

For Camus, theatre was the highest art form. It was also a form of home. 'Why I work in the theatre?' was a subject he would later address in a television series put together by Pierre Cardinal and broadcast in May 1959. Camus set about answering the question in a bullish way which, he suspected, might disappoint his audience: 'quite simply because a stage set is one of the places in the world where I am happy' (*oc*, IV, 603). Still bearing the scars from the debate with the Left about engaged literature and the bourgeois retreat from social commitment, Camus was in effect dismissing the objection of those who complained that to be happy was to exclude those living in misery. Indeed he asserted that the experience of private pleasure could equip the individual to address public need.

At the time of the television interview in May 1959, Camus was putting on at the Théâtre Antoine in Paris an adaptation of Dostoyevsky's *The Possessed*, which he would go on to take to Venice in July of that year. Nostalgia fed into the brio with which Camus set about his theatre interview with Pierre Cardinal.

Camus directing Faulkner's *Requiem for a Nun* at the Théâtre des Mathurins, Paris, 1956.

He traced his involvement in drama back to the days of the Théâtre du Travail in 1936, when he helped assemble a makeshift troupe that put on performances ranging from Aeschylus to Malraux and Dostoyevsky in a popular dance hall – the Bains Padovani on the waterfront in Algiers.

The teenage Camus, seated front row and sporting a goalkeeper's cap, in the Racing Universitaire d'Alger junior football team.

How was it, Camus wondered, that this 'intoxication' had lasted so long? 'Through theatre I escape from what bores me in my craft as a writer' (*oc*, IV, 604), he confessed to his audience, explaining that he wanted away from 'frivolous obstruction'. By this he meant the frustration that came with being a public figure: 'you spend a fair bit of your time resisting invitations to waste it.' The antidote to the frivolity that came with celebrity was putting on a play, he explained, since the endless rehearsals stretching into the night meant an ideal escape: 'It's paradise. From that point of view, the theatre is my convent' (*oc*, IV, 605). Years before in the port of Algiers, the young Camus, employed by a shipping agent, had felt seduced by the quasi-monastic allure of the cramped living quarters of sailors on board ship. Working for the stage rekindled that enthusiasm: 'For two months . . . a community of worker-monks, removed from the world, prepares the sacred office to be celebrated one evening for the first time' (*oc*, IV, 605).

Camus also settled some old scores in his 'Why I work in the theatre?' interview. He contrasted his experience of the theatre with the world of intellectuals, where he had felt the need to be forever apologizing for himself. Working with actors had allowed him to be the person he was ('je suis naturel'). He was unapologetic in his defence of camaraderie, 'one of the great joys of my life which I lost when I left a newspaper we had run as a team and which I found again as soon as I went back to theatre' (*oc*, IV, 606). The career of writing, he continued, condemned one to isolation: 'A writer is judged in solitude and is especially his own judge in solitude' (*oc*, IV, 606). Unsurprisingly, he expressed a Romantic longing for history's communities of builders and for the Renaissance with its painters working together in collectives.

The materiality of the stage entranced Camus as much, he recalled, as did the experience of standing at the marble stone on which the pages of a newspaper were set – a world away from the writing of the 'sermons we call editorials'. Who was it, Camus asked, who said that to be a good stage director, one had to feel with one's arms the weight of the objects that made up the set? He dismissed the view that theatre was an escapist medium, objecting that one finds more actors and posers in salons and places of government than on the stage. Indeed in the interdependence whereby actors and directors needed each other, Camus saw a levelling principle not without value to future societies (*oc*, IV, 606).

If Camus risked idealizing the world of stagecraft in his 'Why I work in the theatre?' interview, photographs of him directing nevertheless show a figure who is intensely absorbed and often exhilarated. The relish of collective endeavour was very real for him. As a boy growing up in working-class Belcourt he was already familiar with the culture of the street and the solidarity among workers at the small factory where Etienne Sintès, his uncle, was employed. This early exposure to communal living and his romancing of teamwork throws into relief the dread he came to associate with literary composition in solitude. Back in his mid-teens, playing as goalkeeper for the junior side at the Racing Universitaire d'Alger football club gave him as much pleasure as would the theatre later. (Before the RUA days, it was a football made of rags and an improvised match on a parade ground in Algiers with Muslim and French boys (*FM*, 185).) As Camus remarked in what has become an often-cited line, 'The little bit of morality I know I learnt on football pitches and stage sets and they will remain my real universities' (*OC*, IV, 607).

13

Stockholm and the Backdrop to Fame

I share that misery and his face is the face of my country.

Camus (*oc*, IV, 289)

Ten years after André Gide had received the award and five years on from the success of François Mauriac in 1952, Camus was in Stockholm in December 1957 to receive the Nobel Prize for Literature. He was quick to tell journalists when news of the award came out on 16 October that André Malraux was a more accomplished writer and would have made a more deserving recipient. There was no guile in this position. Malraux had a long-established record as one of France's leading novelists and indeed had opened doors for the young Camus back in 1941 when he gave the go-ahead at Gallimard for the publication of *The Outsider* and *The Myth of Sisyphus*.

In the lofty terms of the Nobel citation, Camus' work highlighted the problems that presented themselves to the human conscience of his day. Privately, he was uneasy. He wrote in his diary on 17 October 1957: 'Nobel. Strange feeling of exhaustion and melancholy. Aged 20, poor, and naked, I experienced true glory. My mother' (*oc*, IV, 1266). The prize came at a time when Camus' standing among many Parisian intellectuals was low. René Char loyally hailed the news as 'the best day in a long time for me among so many days of despair' and sent Camus a keepsake from his time in the Resistance (a small box which, Char said, had helped save his life).[1] He also sang Camus' praises in the *Figaro littéraire* on 26 October in a piece entitled 'Je veux parler d'un ami' (I want to speak about a friend).[2]

Camus knew that the Nobel award would provoke animosity in some quarters, noting in his diary in the days after the announcement the 'low attacks' made against him. Among the most hostile reactions were right-wing voices such as that of the writer Lucien Rebatet, whose death sentence at the end of the Second World War for collaboration had been commuted. Rebatet railed against the 'sterility' and 'outmoded' character of the laureate's work and referred sarcastically to its author's role in the purges at the end of the Second World War. While Camus had initially supported the policy of purging, he had joined others in calling for clemency for Rebatet. And he would go on to concede, as we saw in an earlier chapter, that Mauriac's position on the question of retribution had been the right one.[3]

Camus was to make good what he saw as his error with his powerful advocacy of an end to the death penalty in his essay *Réflexions sur la guillotine* (Reflections on the Guillotine). This was published in the autumn of 1957 together with Arthur Koestler's parallel analysis of the situation obtaining in Britain, *Réflexions sur la potence* (Reflections on the Gallows).[4] It was to the future that Camus appealed to deliver a ban on capital punishment, arguing that in the united Europe that was to come, the solemn abolition of such a practice should be the first article of the European code. (Robert Badinter was the Minister in France responsible for the banning of the death penalty in 1981, a policy that is now a requirement of membership of the European Union.)

In his 1957 essay Camus branded the practice of death by guillotine a 'disgusting butchery' and a 'coarse surgery' (*oc*, IV, 166–7). Capital punishment went against 'the only indisputable human solidarity, solidarity against death' (*oc*, IV, 159) and his goal was to 'show the obscenity that lies behind the cloak of words' (*oc*, IV,

Francine and Albert Camus at the time of the announcement of his Nobel Prize in Literature, 1957.

128). Camus also thought about the problem laterally. That many homicides were alcohol-related prompted his pithy formulation: 'The State . . . limits itself to cutting off heads into which it itself has poured so much wine' (*oc*, IV, 150).

Political violence during the Algerian War saw the French government make extensive use of the death penalty with the first state executions of Algerian insurrectionaries dating from June

The Barberousse (now Serkadji) Prison in Algiers in an earlier decade. Camus'
father witnessed a public execution there and was deeply shaken by the spectacle.
The knowledge of his father's revulsion helped shape Camus' opposition to the
death penalty.

1956. This violence in turn led to an increase in FLN attacks against
civilian targets in Algiers.[5] Camus made numerous interventions in
private, seeking to have verdicts of execution handed down to
Algerian rebels commuted. In a letter of April 1961 to Pierre Nora,
who had written in hostile terms of Camus' position on Algeria,
Jacques Derrida would argue that behind the scenes Camus had
been more intensely exercised about the use of the death penalty
than were many of those who were more ostensibly engaged with
the conflict.[6]

Welcoming the news of the Nobel Prize in *Le Monde* (18 October
1957), Edouard Henriot described Camus as a 'public director of
conscience' who had served to fill the void at the level of principles
and beliefs left by the events of the Second World War and cited
The Rebel as his greatest achievement. Henriot also greeted the
award as an honour for France at a time when it was weakened
and criticized. The narrative of national weakness was code for the

situation in Algeria. The FLN had been working to internationalize
the conflict and to set out its case for independence. The United
Nations called on France to seek a 'non-violent, democratic and
just' solution to the conflict in Algeria. The then U.S. Senator John
F. Kennedy spoke along similar lines on 2 July 1957.[7]

France's use of military force in Algeria had been unrelenting,
most conspicuously during what came to be known as *la Bataille
d'Alger* (the Battle of Algiers). Working to combat the FLN bombing
of civilian targets in the capital, General Massu's paratroopers had
swamped the Kasbah, the old Muslim citadel, in January 1957.
In the months that followed, torture was used systematically in an
attempt to quell the upsurge in FLN violence. Under the massive
French military presence, thousands of Algerian Muslims were
disappeared.

Much more publicity however was given to what were to
become high-profile cases involving French Algerian supporters
of the Algerian insurrection. Maurice Audin, a teaching assistant
at the University of Algiers and member of the Algerian
Communist Party, died (it later emerged) on 21 June 1957 as a
result of torture at the hands of French paratroopers who claimed
that he was on the run having escaped from custody.[8] Another
high-profile case involved Henri Alleg, who had been director of
Alger républicain (Camus' old paper) from 1950 until it was shut
down by the government in 1955. Alleg had been tortured by
French paratroopers in a civilian prison in the El Biar district of
Algiers. A high-profile press campaign forced the authorities to
present Alleg to an examining magistrate on 17 August 1957. When
the story of his torture came to be published in Paris by the
Editions de Minuit in January 1958, *La Question* (The Question), as
it was entitled, provoked intense interest. Alleg launched his narrative with a quotation from Romain Rolland's novel *Jean-Christophe* –
'When I attack those French who are corrupt, I am defending
France' – and ended by explaining to those in France who were

prepared to read his testimony that his aim was to inform them about 'what is being done here IN THEIR NAME'.[9]

This appeal to France and the French against the actions of other French was feeding into a broader fracture. It was not just figures on the Left who were expressing their opposition to torture, even if *Les Temps modernes* under Sartre's direction was a vociferous channel for such opposition. Paul Teitgen, secretary general of police in Algiers, resigned from his post in September 1957 in protest at what he saw as evidence of the same torture which he himself had undergone at the hands of the Gestapo in Nancy in eastern France fourteen years earlier.[10] François Mauriac had already raised moral concerns about French military tactics in *L'Express* back in January 1955 in an article entitled 'La Question'. He was to continue to voice unease along with other writers of religious persuasion such as Pierre-Henri Simon, whose pamphlet *Contre la torture* (Against Torture) appeared in 1957. From September of that year, as Benjamin Stora explains, wide divergences appeared between France's political leadership and its military, between metropolitan France and the French Algerians, and within the Left politically.[11]

This culture of schism and recrimination necessarily impacted on Camus' own position as a public figure of French Algerian origin who had consistently called for measures to address social and economic injustices. Crucially, the proposed scope of such measures was now coming to have less purchase with the spiral into a war that was to see the enforced displacement of two million Algerian Muslim peasants in the French Army's pursuit of the war against the military wing of the FLN, the ALN (Army of National Liberation). With more radical solutions being called for, Camus saw his position being eroded. A number of former allies now supported calls for Algerian independence. Ferhat Abbas, for example, the leader of the moderate UDMA, the 'Union Démocratique du manifeste algérien' (Democratic Union of the Algerian Manifesto), had aligned himself with the FLN.

On 1 October 1957 Camus met the ethnographer Germaine Tillion in Paris to discuss Algeria. She recounted her meeting in the Kasbah in Algiers with leaders of the FLN with whom she discussed their bombing of civilian targets in the city and the state execution of militants. Tillion reported on the schoolwork which she had seen of eleven- and twelve-year-old Algerian pupils who had been invited by their teacher to reflect on what they would do if they were invisible: the children wrote of their desire to take up arms against French paratroopers, the French and the French government. Faced with this mounting evidence of irreversible social fracture, Camus wrote in his diary: 'I despair of the future' (*oc*, IV, 1266).

Algiers, 1957: French troops patrolling the Casbah during the Algerian War of Independence.

Writing in October 1957, Tillion herself reflected on the radical turn of events in a study in which she presented France and Algeria as 'complementary enemies' and which she first published the following year.[12] She explained to her readers that, in an analysis she had published some time earlier, she might have given the impression that economic measures would resolve Algeria's difficulties. This was a misunderstanding, she now reflected, as was any more recent belief that the application of 'exclusively political medication' would work. Such a view was, in Tillion's words, 'chimerical': 'the disease is probably fatal', she concluded.[13]

It was inevitable that the critical situation in Algeria would find its way into the exchanges surrounding Camus' Stockholm visit in December 1957. In his acceptance speech he referred to the unfinished nature of his work and expressed the emotion he felt on receiving a prize at a time when writers in certain parts of Europe (the example of Boris Pasternak in the Soviet Union was one such case) faced persecution and when his native Algeria was living through *un malheur incessant* (an unending misery) (*oc*, IV, 239).

Camus went on to explain that while he could not live without his art, such a position in no way isolated him: art submitted the artist to 'the most humble and universal truth'. By the same logic, the writer, he continued, was available not to those 'who make history' but to those 'who are subjected to it' (*oc*, IV, 240). Thus the oppressed prisoner at the other end of the world draws the writer out of his isolation and restores him to the reality of community. In a form of generational self-portrait, Camus appealed to the life-experience of his contemporaries, those born around the time of the First World War who went on to live through National Socialism and the early trials in the Soviet Union in the 1930s, the Second World War and the threat of nuclear destruction (*oc*, IV, 241).

Writing just over two years later in the wake of Camus' death, the Algerian novelist Mohammed Dib, as if to offer a reprise of

Camus' characterization of his generation, would record his regret that Camus' work should convey a sense of unredeemed pessimism. He argued that his friend had come into 'a world in ruins, a world flavoured with cinders and the sun, in which man is no longer even a survivor but already a shadow of Hiroshima man'.[14] Camus, Dib added, had created a world dominated not just by the death of God but by the death of man, with no prospect of alleviation. This, for Dib, accounted for the 'sombre greatness and the weakness' of the work.

Both Dib and Camus then make the case for the latter's pessimism while differing in substantial measure on the question of its degree. The Nobel acceptance speech shows a public figure wrestling with paradox, as when Camus describes the writer as being 'vulnerable but stubborn', torn 'between suffering and beauty' and confronted with 'the destructive movement of history' (*oc*, IV, 242). Camus concluded that it would be naive to expect from the writer ready-made solutions and uplifting moral pronouncements. His tone was both penitential (he spoke of 'my errors', 'my faults', 'my limits') and defiant (he claimed that he would share the struggle of the persecuted who, unlike him, had received no privilege). As if to underscore the language of moral ambiguity, he described the writer as being – along with others engaged in the struggle – 'unjust and passionate about justice'.

The pomp and circumstance of the Stockholm visit provided no immunity from controversy. In a meeting with students in Stockholm on the afternoon of 12 December, Camus spoke about the situation in Hungary where Soviet troops had put down an uprising a year earlier. He then went on to talk about Algeria. A young Algerian supporter of the FLN asked why it was that Camus was outspoken about repression in Eastern Europe and yet refused to condemn French actions in Algeria.

The country was de facto in a state of war. By 1957 the French army, largely made up of conscripts, had 400,000 troops serving there. The use of state torture was clear from the high-profile cases of, first, General de la Bollardière and then (as mentioned earlier) the Algiers police chief Paul Teitgen, both of whom had asked that year to be relieved of their commands because of their opposition to the practice.

The altercation that ensued between Camus and the FLN sympathizer was reported in the French press. The supporter of the FLN defended the movement's methods and publicly berated Camus. In his reply Camus pointed out that he was the only journalist to have been expelled from Algeria – this not long after he had exposed the plight of the Kabyles back in 1939 – and alluded to private interventions which he had made to help save the lives of a number of FLN members sentenced to death. He concluded:

> I have always condemned the use of [state] terror. I must also condemn a terrorism that acts blindly, in the streets of Algiers, for example, and which could one day strike my mother or my family. I believe in justice, but I will defend my mother before justice (*OC*, IV, 288–9).

It was the last of these sentences, taken in isolation, which was seen as incendiary back in Algeria and France. For many, it served to pigeonhole Camus: it was read as an implicit endorsement of the French military's repressive role, as an expression of indifference to the imperatives of a wider social justice. Camus' phrasing had been maladroit when he presented the pursuit of justice and the safety of his mother in the FLN's bombing campaign against the civilian population of Algiers as being somehow mutually exclusive. Yet his intention was never to endorse French military repression – his rejection of state terror in the same breath had made that clear.

Further controversy surrounded the misreporting of another of Camus' remarks. Asked about the extent of press censorship in respect of events in Algeria, he had expressed the view that restrictions, in metropolitan France at least, had been minimal. *Le Monde* reported however that it was French military interventions in Algeria that Camus had described in such terms. The impact was explosive.

Camus complained to the management of *Le Monde* that his comments had been misrepresented and that his view of the record of the French army was quite different from the one attributed to him. The newspaper promptly issued a correction but the damage had already been done. *France Observateur* ran with the same story, featuring a piece entitled 'From Sisyphus to Lacoste', the suggestion being that Camus now occupied the role of Robert Lacoste, the governor general of Algeria who had been appointed in February 1956 to appease French Algerian opinion. Writing to the editor of *France Observateur* on 20 December 1957, Camus expressed his disgust and demanded a public retraction (*oc*, IV, 291).

At the private level, he castigated his friend, the gay European Algerian poet Jean Sénac in a letter of 19 December 1957 for what Camus saw as Sénac's indecent haste – 'Quelle hâte, Sénac!' (*oc*, IV, 290) – in believing what *Le Monde* had originally printed. Like Camus, Sénac had a mother of Spanish origins. And like Camus, he had grown up in urban poverty, in Sénac's case in the Saint-Eugène district of Oran. But on the question of Algerian independence, they were on opposing sides. An aggrieved Camus offered what he termed 'a final piece of advice from an old friend', namely that Sénac, if he wished to speak in terms of 'love and fraternity', should stop writing poetry which glorified FLN violence and in particular 'the bomb which indiscriminately kills the child and the awful, "unseeing" adult'. Camus ended his letter by expressing misgivings about his own work while asserting that Sénac's apology for political violence robbed the poet's work of its validity.

The disparity of outlook between Camus and his fellow European Algerian writer, whose work he had earlier published in the Gallimard Espoir series, was captured in a then unpublished poem of Sénac's dated 1–15 September 1956 carrying a dedication 'A Albert Camus qui me traitait d'égorgeur' (To Albert Camus who called me a cut-throat). Sénac writes of 'the Master of the Absolute' (the allusion is to Camus) who talks about Man (and not men) and who seeks to occupy a position of purity in a world of bloody conflict: 'Who will wash us clean, says the Master of the Absolute, which Mediterranean will wash away so much mud?'[15] Sénac contrasts this position with that of the Poet who suggests to the Master of the Absolute that 'Between men and you, blood is flowing . . . and you no longer see.'[16] The tone of personal reproach becomes more diffuse in another of Sénac's poems, 'Au nom du peuple' . . . (In the Name of the People . . .) in which he uses a formulation akin to Alleg's closing line in *The Question*: 'what is being done here IN THEIR NAME'. In Sénac's poem, which lists French atrocities, 'In the Name of the French People' becomes a mantra.[17]

Sénac's own life was to end in his violent death in post-independence Algeria in 1973. But the painful rift between him and Camus in December 1957 was symptomatic of the social fracturing brought about by the Algerian War. Stockholm therefore meant no easy canonization for Camus. His public pronouncements in Sweden and the reporting of these back home came to be read principally through the prism of Algeria.

Tellingly, when he called on the French press to correct its misreporting of his remarks, Camus took the opportunity to restate his mistrust of metropolitan attitudes. To the editor of *Le Monde* he wrote that he felt closer to the young Algerian supporter of the FLN who had confronted him in Stockholm on the question of justice than to many French people who spoke of Algeria, he insisted, with no knowledge of the country. Of his Algerian interlocutor, Camus wrote: 'his face was not one of hatred but of despair and misery. I share that misery and his face is the face of my country' (*OC*, IV, 289).

In an interview given on the eve of the conferring of the Nobel Prize, the aspiration to forge a Franco-Algerian community had featured. Asked about its feasibility, Camus confirmed that such a co-existence was not only possible but necessary. And in reply to a question about his relations with young Algerian writers, he noted that it was precisely these literary connections which proved that such a community was possible. Alongside European writers such as himself, Emmanuel Roblès and Jules Roy, Camus listed Mohammed Dib (who would go on to be Algeria's leading literary figure of the century) and the Kabyle writers Mouloud Mammeri and Mouloud Feraoun (*oc*, IV, 280).

Feraoun was a friend of Germaine Tillion, whose ethnographic fieldwork had seen her spend over six years in Algeria prior to the Second World War and who had been making numerous visits there on behalf of the French government in the years after 1954. Tillion would write of 'the great bleeding ulcer Algeria has become'.[18] On 15 March 1962 Feraoun was assassinated by the right-wing terrorist group the Organisation de l'Armée secrète (OAS, Secret Army Organization), which stood for the maintenance of French Algerian supremacy. He was one of six inspectors killed that day in social centres which Tillion had seen set up as part of a French attempt to improve literacy and living conditions more generally for the Algerian Muslim population. In the months that followed, the mass exodus of the great majority of the European Algerian population would take place, with over 930,000 leaving the country in the course of 1962.[19]

To the end of his life in early 1960, Camus had held on to the belief that after the killings of the Algerian War, the native Algerian populations and the European settler population would have to find a way to resume their cohabitation. Yet the events of the war were to lead to full independence, an outcome he had not envis-aged. Nor had Germaine Tillion when she wrote: 'Frenchmen and Algerians – it is impossible to conceive of two populations whose mutual dependence is more certain.'[20]

14

1958

Two rights have been forgotten in the Declaration of the Rights of
Man: the right to contradict oneself and the right to go away.
Charles Baudelaire[1]

Stockholm had been a test of resilience. By the end of it, Camus
wrote with relief to Jean Grenier: 'The corrida is just about to
finish, with the bull dead, or not far from it.'[2] Away from the lime-
light and the controversy, things were not well in Camus' private
life. He had been suffering from acute anxiety and in his diary in
late 1957 he recorded details of panic attacks and claustrophobia:
'For a few minutes sensation of total madness. Then exhaustion
and trembling. Tranquillizers . . . Night of 29–30 [December]:
interminable anxiety' (*oc*, IV, 1267). In the spring of 1958, he noted
the steps to be taken in his attempt to get back to health:

Stages of a healing.
Let the will subside. Enough of 'I must'.
Depoliticize the mind totally in order to humanize. . . .
Address the question of death, that's to say accept it . . .
(*oc*, IV, 1271)

Some lines from Nietzsche seemed to offer a way forward.
Camus noted the philosopher's observation that the fear of death
was 'a European disease' and he seemed intrigued by Nietzsche's

portrait of the man of the future, 'eccentric, energetic, warm, indefatigable, an artist, enemy of books' (*oc*, IV, 1270). There was an acknowledgement by Camus that in his own case a whole way of being and doing had to change: 'Need to break systematically the automatic reflexes from the smallest to the biggest. Tobacco, food, sex, emotional reactions of defence (or of attack – they amount to the same thing) and *creation itself* (*oc*, IV, 1272). Camus' use of italicization highlighted the radical prospect of his suppressing the core activity of his career as an artist. His writing had virtually ground to a halt. Yet like the artist Jonas in *Exile and the Kingdom*, he was experiencing the paradox of fame and private stagnation: 'as luck would have it, the less [Jonas] worked, the greater his reputation grew' (*EK*, 67).

Camus was desperate to shed the burden of solitude that came with the work of written composition. The frenetic pace of his life – losing himself in endless activity, his affairs, his intense involvement in political and ideological engagements – suggested an intense restlessness which has been read by at least one commentator as evidence that he was in flight from psychological trauma.[3]

March 1958 saw the republication, this time by Gallimard, of *L'Envers et l'Endroit*, the slim volume which Edmond Charlot had first brought out in Algiers back in 1937. Camus provided a preface for the new edition. If he was at low ebb given the hostility he faced over Algeria, the preface allowed him to vent his frustration as a French Algerian looking in on cultural power in France. It was the memory of the truths glimpsed in *L'Envers et l'Endroit*, he argued, that had prevented him from being at ease in 'the public exercise of my craft' (*oc*, I, 35). 'Here are my people, my masters, this is my lineage' (*oc*, I, 37), he asserted in a tone that was both defensive and combative. He further complained of the vanity of the cultural scene in the capital where all was 'envy and derision' (*oc*, I, 35) and condemned the cultural arrogance implicit in the *Tout Paris* (literally 'All of Paris') label which served to denote nothing other than a small social elite. He declared himself humbled by both society's poor and the 'great adventures of the mind' undertaken by the likes of Melville, Tolstoy and Nietzsche – what fell in between was risible, he objected. He preferred to skip the social circus – the opening nights for plays and French society's 'love-ins' around works and their authors in which admiration flowed, he quipped, as freely as Pernod or as the letters that poured into the problem pages of daily newspapers.

With its brooding tone, the preface to *L'Envers et l'Endroit* saw Camus dismiss his critics in metropolitan France and shape a retrospective on a series of early short prose narratives which he saw as laying the foundations for his writing career. To draw again on Camus' verdict on the collection, 'there is more true love in these awkward pages than in all those that have followed' (*OC*, I, 31–2). Camus was now holding up the writing that had come out of life in Belcourt as a form of riposte to Saint-Germain-des-Prés.

Yet the mood of defensiveness pointed to a wounded soul. In the same preface, he worked to throw off a reputation which had always frustrated him, that of being the voice of moral conscience. Yes, Camus conceded, he had often stressed the need to strive for justice but he insisted that in his own life he had often failed: 'Man sometimes strikes me as an injustice on the move: I am thinking of myself' (*OC*, I, 37). Perhaps the only recourse, he suggested, was to live according to honour, 'that virtue of the unjust!' (*OC*, I, 37). But in an ironic aside, Camus checked himself, recalling how in philosophical and literary circles – and again he had the left-wing Paris intelligentsia in his sights – honour had become a dirty word with connotations of aristocratic aloofness.

Camus' continuing belief, which he had restated in Stockholm, that the formation of a Franco-Algerian community could deliver a way out of conflict was to be confounded by the momentous public events of 1958. On a trip home to Algeria in March, he focused – as he had done when writing 'Summer in Algiers' back in the 1930s –

on those he referred to as his people, noting again the emphasis they placed on family and friendship and bodily pleasure: 'a life whose only horizon is their immediate needs . . . Proud of their virility, of their ability to eat and drink, of their strength and courage. Vulnerable' (*oc*, IV, 1271). Camus could see the weakness behind the *bonhomie*. On the passenger ferry *Kairouan* between Marseilles and Algiers, he also observed the French troops in transit. The conflict was set to reach a new level.

Shortly before his trip home to Algeria, Camus had met De Gaulle in Paris on 5 March and noted afterwards in his diary how the general had dismissed his fears about the prospect of major unrest among French Algerians in the event of the French pulling out of Algeria. De Gaulle had not held political office since 1946 but three months on from this conversation, he was to be back in power. The trigger was North Africa. A group of generals intent on maintaining the status quo in French Algeria attempted a coup on 13 May 1958 and called for the formation of a new national government to be led by De Gaulle. It was a period of intense uncertainty, with the army threatening to take over Paris in what it called Operation Resurrection. In a diary entry for 29 May 1958, Camus wrote cautiously: 'My job is to write my books and to fight when the liberty of my family and my people is threatened. That is all' (*oc*, IV, 1273).

On 1 June De Gaulle became head of government (Président du Conseil, or President of the Council, in the language of the Fourth Republic) and three days later was greeted with adulation in Algiers by those convinced that he would save the day. But who was it that he was addressing when, in his famous opening line to the 100,000-strong crowd gathered outside the Palace of the Government General in Algiers, he uttered the celebrated words, *Je vous ai compris!* (I have understood you!)? French Algerians saw him as their charismatic saviour and yet Muslims in the crowd heard De Gaulle spell out in a very deliberate, methodical manner the message that 'from this day forward, France considers that in the whole of Algeria there is only one category of inhabitant: there are only French in the full sense, French in the full sense, with the same rights and the same duties.'[4]

In what came to be frequently cited words, Camus had commented back in October 1955, in a published letter to Aziz Kessous, that he was 'sick with Algeria . . . just as others are sick in their lungs' – 'j'ai mal à l'Algérie' – adding that his career had shown an intense engagement with the affairs of the country.[5] By the spring of 1958, he was wondering if 'excessive responsibilities' (*oc*, IV, 1272) might not have contributed to his state of mental collapse. In June of that year, Gallimard published *Actuelles III. Chroniques algériennes, 1939–1958* (Algerian Chronicles), which drew together Camus' writings on Algeria: the reporting on famine in Kabylia in June 1939; his work on Algeria for *Combat* at the end of the Second World War; articles published when he returned to journalism with *L'Express* in 1955–6; an intervention on behalf of his friend Jean de Maisonseul who had been arrested in Algiers in 1956 accused of engaging in subversion; and a position piece entitled 'Algérie 1958'.

Camus explained towards the end of his preface, dated March–April 1958, that a number of people had asked him to make his views known. He presented his work as an experience of living in Algeria, as chronicling 'a long confrontation between a man and a situation'. Such a connection, he conceded, brought with it 'all the errors, contradictions and hesitations which such a confrontation implies and of which many examples will be found in the pages that follow' (*oc*, IV, 304). Significantly, Camus commented on people's inflated expectations of the figure of the writer in situations of intractable conflict. In his own case, he reflected, the emotional connection to the country of his birth excluded any possibility of detachment: 'It is vain to believe that such a writer can be the source of a revealed truth' (*oc*, IV, 304).

Far from being mere rhetorical posturing, this was Camus acknowledging his limitations. He insisted that he had no intention of playing to the gallery and he was suspicious of those who argued from a position of intransigence: 'I lack the assurance that allows one to decide categorically' (*oc*, IV, 298). In private he was struggling to recover from a breakdown and part of the therapy, as we have seen, was to 'depoliticize the mind totally in order to humanize' (*oc*, IV, 1271).

In his *Algerian Chronicles* preface, Camus rehearsed the constraints and risks facing those in his position. If he criticized the Algerian rebellion, those responsible for colonial wrongdoing would feel morally justified; and if he focused exclusively on the wrongs of French colonial rule, he would give succour to the FLN whose bombing campaign in civilian areas was placing at risk those members of his family still living in Algiers – 30 September 1956 had seen the first FLN bomb attacks in Algiers, with two busy cafes, the Milk-bar and the Cafétéria, among the targets.[6]

Camus may have been living in France since the Second World War but his emotional investment in the Algerian conflict was intense and he was desperate to avoid writing from, as he termed it, the 'comfort of a study'. He saw FLN violence and French military repression as the drivers in a cycle of violence and he rejected both. Predicting repressive, single-party military rule in any post-independence Algeria, he called for a Commonwealth-style federal solution to the France–Algeria conflict. He was categorical that he would refuse to assist Algerian independence in any way and complained of a broader, pan-Arab movement directed from Egypt by the country's leader, Gamal Abdel Nasser.

Targeting the liberal intellectual consensus in France, which was now increasingly unsympathetic to the French Algerian position, Camus contrasted the movement towards decolonization in the West in the wake of the Second World War with the expansion of the Soviet Union through its absorption of numerous states in central and Eastern Europe.

With the war in Algeria bringing acute polarization, his position came to be increasingly marginal and he concluded *Algerian Chronicles* by signalling that this would be his final pronouncement on the situation there. Both metropolitan liberals and right-wing elements in the French Algerian population disowned him. On the indigenous Algerian side, he had been perturbed years earlier in a meeting with Algerian nationalists in Tlemcen around about 1946 when they told him that European settlers seeking to bring about reform were the nationalists' worst enemy: 'You weaken us in our will to struggle', they had objected (*oc*, III, 933). The FLN now dismissed *Algerian Chronicles* as, in the words of Ahmed Taleb, an FLN prisoner held in Fresnes jail, a work of bad faith full of fine-sounding phrases.[7]

Coverage of *Algerian Chronicles* in France was thin and often negative. Jean Lacouture, writing in *Le Monde*, expressed frustration at Camus' desire to position himself as an arbiter in what was 'a demented dialogue between paralytics and epileptics'. Raymond Aron, a public intellectual on the Right, had supported the idea of Algerian independence back in 1956. He now criticized *Algerian Chronicles* for failing to take on board the legitimacy of the nationalist position.[8]

One of the people Camus spent time with on his trip to Algeria in March 1958 was the Kabyle novelist and schoolteacher Mouloud Feraoun. They had started corresponding shortly after Feraoun's first novel, *Le Fils du pauvre* (The Poor Man's Son), was published in 1950. On Camus' spring 1958 visit, Feraoun brought him along to his classes; they discussed the war and together visited a shantytown inhabited by Muslims. Later, Camus would write to his friend: 'I have come to hope for a more genuine future, I mean one in which we shall be separated neither by injustice nor by justice.'[9]

Mouloud Feraoun, Berber writer and friend of Camus.

Feraoun set out his response to *Algerian Chronicles* in an open letter to Camus which he published in September 1958.[10] Noting with regret that little attention had been paid to the volume, Feraoun observed that for him personally Camus' articles on hunger in Kabylia back in 1939 had been revelatory: 'You were very young', he wrote,

> when the plight of the Muslim populations was already a source of concern for you . . . When I read your articles in *Alger républicain*, the newspaper of the schoolteachers, I said to myself: 'There's one decent guy' (Voilà un brave type). I admired your tenacity in wanting to understand, your curiosity which grew

out of sympathy and perhaps love. I felt you to be so close to me then, so fraternal and totally lacking in prejudice.[11]

But Feraoun's praise of Camus was also a call for radical change from someone who had lost faith in the system of cultural assimilation which had seen him become a primary school teacher formed in the French republican mould. He explained that back in 1939, he and fellow Muslims felt they were the vanquished, whereas 'your ones were using more than ever the language of the conquerors.' Feraoun recalled what happened to Camus in the wake of his reporting on Kabylia: how, after his protest, Camus was driven out of the country, being seen as more dangerous than the vanquished.[12]

Feraoun's fraternal endorsement of Camus is further reflected when he cites a page from 'Destitution in Kabylia' on the subject of the provision of education as 'the most solemn warning that a man of compassion and courage could have given to his country'.[13] Yet Feraoun also pinpointed the limits of French republican discourse. It was the error of the French, he observed, 'to have tried to turn Algerians into French people'.[14] He went on to highlight the discrepancy whereby the democracy that had allowed Camus to ask for justice was for Muslims a tyranny. Nevertheless, the tone of utopian aspiration in 'Destitution in Kabylia' had moved Feraoun, as when Camus anticipated the day when the children of Algeria would share the same school benches and 'two peoples made to understand each other will begin to know each other', peoples, Feraoun comments, who for a century and more were connected by 'that inhuman commerce which links the weak to the strong . . . the servant to the master'.[15]

Camus was not optimistic. Writing from Paris to Jean Grenier on 4 August 1958, he reflected that 'it was doubtless too late for Algeria', although he added that history can take unexpected turns.[16] In October De Gaulle launched plans for economic and social reform and offered the FLN *la paix des braves* (the peace of the brave); the FLN rejected this call to lay down their arms. Yet De Gaulle's move may have caused Camus to wonder if his own writing on Algeria might add to the reformist momentum. In November he rang his close friend Michel Gallimard to ask if, in the light of the new political direction, the title page of *Actuelles III* could be modified. Camus wanted *Chroniques algériennes* to feature in large red capitals as the new title of the volume with perhaps a reduced font-size for *Actuelles III*.[17] While the changes to the title page were implemented and suggested a writer who longed to exert some influence on the situation in Algeria, the work itself was dwarfed by events.

For a number of years Camus and his family had holidayed in the Vaucluse region of southeast France. The landscape there reminded him of his native Algeria. His friendship with René Char, which developed after the war, was part of this link to the region. Char had fought in the Resistance and had a home in L'Isle sur la Sorgue. For Camus he was the leading poet of his day and one who had shown, Camus wrote, that one can 'fight for beauty as well as for one's daily bread'.[18] *Feuillets d'Hypnos* (Leaves of Hypnos), a collection of poetry reflecting Char's involvement in the Resistance, appeared as part of Camus' Espoir collection in 1946.

Char did not need convincing about Camus' restlessness in Paris. He himself had confided to Camus back in September 1948: 'I despise Paris . . . that strange magnet.'[19] In the wake of the row that engulfed *The Rebel* in 1952, he extended a poetic invitation to Camus and his wife to rediscover nature:

Dear Francine, Dear Albert, The antidote to the tree used in the buildings of Paris is the seasonal tree of the forest . . . I can't wait to see you both, couple of my thought. With all my affection, René Char.[20]

Camus' own frustration with metropolitan living was a regular refrain. In September 1946 he confided to Louis Guilloux that he would like to leave the capital and pursue his work in the countryside but that financial constraints prevented this.[21] Paris, he would later write, was a place 'where the sun is a luxury, where dying costs an arm and a leg, and where there are no trees that don't have a bank account. Paris which wants to give lessons to the world'.[22]

Given his state of psychological anxiety in the early months of 1958, Camus was keener than ever to get away. In June he went to Greece for a month with Maria Casares and Michel and Janine Gallimard, visiting the Cyclades Islands. He wrote to Grenier about the appeal of the archipelago which reminded him of the content of the 'Iles Fortunées' (Fortunate Isles) chapter in Grenier's *Les Iles*.[23] Camus added that 'the sea washes everything.'

In late August, Char was in touch about a house in Cabrières d'Avignon which the Camus family had arranged to rent while they searched for a place in the area: 'You will find a natural peace there fit for a king', he promised.[24] A few days later, Camus was recording his enthusiasm for the region, describing a long drive with Char in the Luberon hills: 'I was transported by the violent light, the infinite space. Yet again I would like to live here, find the house that suits me, and finally settle a bit' (*oc*, IV, 1289–90). Soon after, with the money from the Nobel Prize, the Camus family acquired an attractive house in the village of Lourmarin. It was September. Camus was keen to send news of the house purchase in the Grand'rue de l'Eglise (known today as the rue Albert Camus) to Jean Grenier, who had been introduced to the village by the writer Henri Bosco and was married there in 1928.[25] Camus himself had stayed in Lourmarin with Jules Roy and Jean Amrouche back in 1946, noting then in his diary that it was 'A solemn and austere region – in spite of its striking beauty'.[26] About the same visit he enthused to Louis Guilloux in a letter of 24 October 1946: 'For three days, I was walking on those hills and in that light with such joy. When I was there, I forgot about everything.'[27] Little wonder that when he dedicated a copy of *La Peste* to close friends of René Char in the region, the inscription read: 'To Mme Roux and Doctor Roux, this homage to medicine . . . with the faithful thought of someone proud to call himself a Vauclusian.'[28] By the autumn of 1958, putting down roots in Lourmarin had become increasingly important for a writer trying to work out his future direction.

15

Cohabiting with Oneself

I do not guide anyone.

Camus[1]

Camus' writing in the last months of 1958 had virtually dried up.
He produced some short occasional pieces: for *Le Figaro littéraire* a
defence of Boris Pasternak, whose *Doctor Zhivago* had been banned
in the Soviet Union and who declined the Nobel Prize in 1958
under pressure from the Soviet authorities; the preface for a book
on the execution of the Hungarian politician Imre Nagy; and
an appeal for donations to help Spanish refugees, published in
Témoins in December 1958. His 45th birthday in November had
been, he recorded in his diary, a day of solitude and reflection, just
as he had wanted it, and he noted the need to develop detachment
(*OC*, IV, 1291). Camus was wary, having vowed to stay out of the
political turmoil surrounding Algeria. A Provisional Government
of the Algerian Republic, the GPRA, under the presidency of Ferhat
Abbas had been formed in Cairo in September 1958 and declared
that 'Algeria was not France.'

Yet involvement in the theatre lifted Camus and he contrasted
this with his struggle to get back into literary composition. He had
invested heavily in his adaptation of *The Possessed* in July and
August 1958. His interest in Dostoyevsky stretched back to the mid-
1930s when at the Théâtre de l'Equipe in Algiers he had enjoyed
playing Ivan Karamazov: 'Perhaps I didn't play the role that well

but it seemed to me that I understood it completely. I was expressing myself directly playing that role', he had reminisced in an interview for *Paris-Théâtre* back in August 1957 (*OC*, IV, 578).

The choice of *The Possessed* for adaptation told its own story and Camus was able to avail himself of a new French translation brought out by Gallimard in 1955. Dostoyevsky had seen his novel as a tendentious work aimed at exposing the demented side of revolutionary discourse and the climate of nihilism which this was spawning in nineteenth-century Russia. Peter Verkhovensky, one of the nihilists, argues that he will destroy everything and that others will build in the wake of the destruction: 'No reform, no amelioration', he warns in the text of Camus' adaptation. Science, the nihilist adds, will sweep away the urge to love; and as for the peasants who work the land, it is not Shakespeare they need but boots (*OC*, IV, 440–41). Camus was comfortable with Dostoyevsky's lampooning of the 'progressives' since this dovetailed with his own critique of the revolutionary Left in the 1950s.[2]

The work also took Camus back to other familiar subjects. The debate conducted by Kirilov around the subject of suicide and life's meaning provided a direct throwback to *The Myth of Sisyphus*. And the crippling guilt and search for atonement embodied by the figure of Stavrogin found a measure of resonance in a number of life stories in Camus' fiction, among them those of Clamence in *The Fall* and Meursault in *The Outsider*. More broadly however, the Dostoyevsky project was re-energizing Camus, who took delight in 'the pleasure in writing, the pleasure in creating, the pleasure in adapting' (*OC*, IV, 552).

Rehearsals for the adaptation began in late 1958 and the play premiered at the Théâtre Antoine in Paris on 30 January 1959. Even after severe cutting, it had a performance time of just under three and a half hours. The premiere in Paris attracted some favourable press coverage although on the Left, *L'Humanité* and *Libération* dismissed the negative depiction of Marxism.[3] But the play was never to achieve the level of acclaim enjoyed by Camus' earlier adaptation of Faulkner.[4] Significantly, however, André Malraux, who was by then De Gaulle's Minister of Culture, was present when the play opened in Paris. Camus was gaining profile as a director. In July 1959 he would spend a week in Venice, where the play began a run at La Fenice that would stretch to almost three months. And later in the year he saw it performed on tour at various locations in France. Back at Gallimard, his secretary, Suzanne Agnely, was expressing dismay that with Camus so drawn to the theatre, he was turning his back on literature.[5] His desire to be given his own theatre to run full-time now seemed achievable. Negotiations for this were under way in the course of 1959 and ironically a letter from Malraux's office dated 4 January 1960, the day Camus died, would confirm plans for a New Theatre which he was to have directed.[6]

The road back into literature was more difficult. In March 1959 Camus complained of fatigue in a letter to Char, reflecting that with youth disappearing, he could no longer muster the strength needed to show insolence or indifference.[7] The loss of confidence added to his sense of withdrawal. On Friday 8 May he wrote to Jean Grenier from Lourmarin, where he stayed for a month. After a term in Paris full of 'work and worries . . . I needed solitude like bread', he confided. He qualified his remark, saying that solitude was his attempt to 'find the path of personal work since all other paths have failed'. He expressed his disgust with what was being currently written, 'the "modern"', the stuff of '"the epoch", as they say', and his gloomy assessment extended to his own published works: 'If I don't find another language, I prefer to remain silent.' Reading Nietzsche's reflections on the figures of Christ and Dionysus, he reflected on the philosopher's troubled mental projections and affirmed that one had to 'be resigned to cohabiting with oneself'.[8] It was as though Camus were invoking 'the right to go away' championed by Baudelaire which had caught his eye twenty years earlier.

Jardin d'Essai, Algiers, 1930s. In *The First Man*, Camus was exploring his early memories of Algiers. One of the attractions of his childhood was the freedom to explore the city's Botanical Gardens, the Jardin d'Essai: 'the children ran on to the huge garden where the rarest of species were raised' (*FM*, 38).

The encounter with self, the 'cohabitation', translated into a fresh attempt at novel-writing, with his family's origins in Algeria as the subject. This was his *First Man* project, the book he had been mulling over for some considerable time and which he was now working on in a concentrated way in 1959 – the unfinished manuscript was found in the wreckage of the car in which he was killed in early January 1960.

Back in 1953 he had given an outline of what would become *The First Man* to Franck Jotterand. In February 1955 he visited Belcourt, again with his family-narrative project in mind. In his diary he gathered details on the family home in Algiers that would filter through into the novel: 'Not a single armchair. A handful of chairs. Nothing changed. No luxuriating nor comfort' (*OC*, IV, 1219).

On the same trip he revisited Tipasa, the ancient Roman site at the foot of the Chenoua mountain that he had originally depicted as a place of innocence in *Nuptials* back in the 1930s. In a 1952 text entitled 'Retour à Tipasa' (Return to Tipasa), he had seen the ancient ruins as being under threat, cordoned off as they were by that stage with barbed wire and drawn into what Camus called a world of 'tyranny, war [and] police' (*OC*, III, 609). He wanted nostalgically to preserve Tipasa as a symbolic counter to European history (*OC*, III, 613). A diary entry marking the February 1955 visit captures the ecological appeal of the site (its flora, the rain and sun, the light) and shows him reinforcing his perception of Tipasa as an antidote to the ugliness of France's industrial cities. Nostalgia was to be foundational to his *First Man* project and the geography of Algeria would come to be worked in as a vehicle for that.

In late March 1959 Camus returned to Algiers to visit his mother, who had undergone an operation. She was the one, he reflected knowingly, 'whose silence has not stopped speaking to me for half of my life', adding that she had lived in ignorance of the world's affairs. She belonged to that group of people 'on whose lives the newspaper, the radio and other technical innovations have had no impact' (*OC*, IV, 1294). Camus would develop the theme of the mother as counterpoint to a turbulent world history in *The First Man* (*FM*, 245). He also took advantage of the trip home to visit Ouled-Fayet, a suburb of Algiers that was his father's birthplace and the place where his parents had been married in November 1909.

The return to his roots was Camus' attempt not just to reaffirm his identity but to rekindle a writing career. This was 'the path of personal work' and what was to remain the unfinished *First Man* would be largely autobiographical. When the novel's hero Jacques Cormery returns to Algiers as an adult, he feels a connection with older family members now deceased. A few 'privileged images', he reflects, reunite him with his family and cancel out what he had tried to be in the intervening years when his career had taken him far from Algiers. It was as though Camus, like his protagonist, was again becoming 'the blind anonymous being that for so many years had survived through his family and that was the source of his true nobility'.[9]

The retreat into anonymity was a marked feature of the late Camus. Towards the end of April 1959, on returning to Lourmarin, he wrote of feeling broken. In May he noted progress on the first part of *The First Man* and evoked with a feeling of gratitude the solitude and beauty of the countryside around Lourmarin (*oc*, IV, 1296).

The First Man also signalled a stylistic retreat. Camus' choice of a naturalist style of composition meant he was working away from 'the "modern"' about which he had been so scathing in his letter of 8 May 1959 to Jean Grenier. A couple of months earlier when back in Algiers, he carried out research at the new Bibliothèque Nationale d'Alger.[10] As he read histories of the French colonial settlement of Algeria, he was drawing on the nineteenth and early twentieth centuries in an effort to forge a cultural identity. In some draft notes for the new project, he described his protagonist as feeling a temporal dislocation brought on by the discovery of his father's war grave in Saint-Brieuc – Camus had visited the burial site with Louis Guilloux in 1947. This 'new order of time' was to provide a framing for the novel but also marked the emotional time in which the writer in Camus was now moving.[11]

In his adaptation of *The Possessed*, the figure of Tikhon had counselled remaining close to one's roots: 'a punishment awaits all those who detach themselves from their native soil, from the truth of a people and a time' (*oc*, IV, 487). As if to heed Tikhon's caution, Camus was choosing Algeria as the backdrop to his writing. His view of the desperateness of the situation in the country was not dissimilar to that expressed by Mouloud Feraoun, who had written of the 'unfathomable tunnel into which we have all been thrown'.[12]

The reality of the Algerian War was filtering through to Camus' draft novel, with glancing references made to young FLN recruits who prefer being in charge, killing and living in the mountains to working as migrant labourers in Béthune in northern France (*FM*, 255), to the detonation of an FLN bomb in an Algiers street and the startled response of Jacques Cormery's mother (*FM*, 58) and to the lynching of four Arabs (*FM*, 232). But Camus' notes also refer to a native Algerian and a European Algerian meeting in Saint-Etienne and to the fraternal bond between these two exiles living in France (*FM*, 230).

With the Algeria of 1959 violently fractured, Camus in what was to be his last novel was willing into being a trans-ethnic, harmonious community. In effect his writing was constructing a parallel world. The opening page of *The First Man* conveys a millennial perspective, with clouds passing overhead almost as slowly as the 'empires and peoples' that had passed through 'this nameless country' (*FM*, 3). In that landscape Camus sets a birth narrative within a Franco-Muslim community that the Algerian War would consign to oblivion. The Muslim cart-driver who transports the pregnant European mother offers a blessing for the baby that is soon to be born (this is a fictional transposition of Camus' own birth in Mondovi in November 1913). Likewise those assisting at the birth, a native Algerian woman and a Madame Jacques, stand at either side of the bed. Outside in the rain, the Algerian cart-driver and the European father take shelter under a sack.

A preoccupied Camus was now reflecting on the force and the source of his writing: 'I am a writer. It is not I but my pen that thinks, remembers and discovers' (*OC*, IV, 1303), he noted in his diary in the latter half of 1959. The same pen was summoning up a world of make-believe, a more tolerable alternative to the mayhem of the war then ravaging Algeria.

While many of his contemporaries parted company with him on the question of the conflict, he remained generous to those on the independence side. One of the FLN leaders, Mohamed Lebjaoui, would later recall that after the failed attempt to bring about a civilian truce in 1956, Camus had striven to understand the aspirations of Algerians and had personally offered to help Lebjaoui if he could.[13] Max-Pol Fouchet, Camus' friend from the early days in Algiers, later wrote that when he declared his opposition to the war in Algeria, Camus, while not agreeing with him, had offered to help: 'If my name can in some way help you . . . I will stand up for you.'[14]

Mindful of metropolitan hostility towards French Algerians, Camus was also stressing in *The First Man* the vulnerability of working-class settler memory. He takes a swipe at the edifice of memory in Proust's novel, commenting that 'remembrance of things past is just for the rich. For the poor it only marks the faint traces on the path to death' (*FM*, 62). He was using the poor families/poor memory nexus to generate narrative pathos in *The First Man*.

On 16 September 1959 De Gaulle announced plans for Algerian self-determination. In June of the previous year, in his famous *Je vous ai compris!* (I have understood you!) address to the vast crowds in Algiers, he had spoken of Algeria having a population of ten million people, all of whom were French. With the prospect in September 1959 of self-determination, native Algerians had the prospect of being heard politically. Camus may have drawn hope from De Gaulle's move, still believing in the possibility of peaceful coexistence between the indigenous communities and the European settler population.[15] Yet *The First Man* describes its protagonist's bemused longing for stronger connection with the country's majority Muslim population:

Around him these people, alluring yet disturbing, near and separate, you were around them all day long, and sometimes friendship was born, or camaraderie, and at evening they still withdrew to their closed houses, where you never entered, barricaded also with their women you never saw, or if you saw them on the street you did not know who they were, with faces half veiled and their beautiful eyes sensual and soft above the white cloth (*FM*, 217).

In this acknowledgement of communities that were adjacent and yet separate, contact with Muslims remains provisional and, indeed, the autonomy of indigenous Algerians awakens anxiety in the European settler.

Camus had campaigned boldly against poverty in Kabylia back in 1939 and had evoked his twenty-year-long engagement with the problems of Algeria when he announced in *Algerian Chronicles* in 1958 that he would adopt a position of silence on the crisis. In his diary he had noted the need to avoid political controversy (*OC*, IV, 1297). His late novel-writing delivered its own mute campaigning, the appendices in the unfinished work proffering an urgent, desperate message with echoes of the Christian Beatitudes:

> Return the land. Give all the land to the poor, to those who have nothing . . . the immense herd of the wretched, mostly Arab and a few French, and who live and survive here through stubbornness and endurance . . . and then I, poor once more and for ever, cast into the worst of exiles at the end of the earth, I will smile and I will die happy, knowing that those I revered, she whom I revered, are at last joined to the land I so loved under the sun where I was born (*FM*, 255).

The 'she' who is revered was an oblique reference to Camus' mother, whom he presents as the emblem of an innocent European Algerian presence.

Yet this redemption narrative could not map on to the reality of late 1950s Algeria. *The First Man*, as Camus himself explained, came out of a temporal dislocation, the one experienced by Jacques Cormery at his father's war grave. Nor did it tell colonial history in a way that was recognizable to indigenous Algerians. In the appendices to the unfinished novel, General Bugeaud is mentioned as bullishly asking the mayor of Toulon to find wives for the twenty French soldiers forming the new settlement of Fouka (Camus' work

in the archive was throwing up this sort of material). The name of
Bugeaud, who led the military subjugation of Algeria in the 1840s,
meant something altogether different to Algerians. Indeed Mouloud
Feraoun recalled in a letter of tribute to Camus in 1958 how in the
1930s the women of the interior, to get their children to be silent,
would warn them: "'Be quiet, Bouchou's coming". Bouchou was
Bugeaud. And Bugeaud was the previous century.'[16]

Over three decades would elapse before *The First Man* reached its
reading public. The circumstances of the Algerian War ruled out any
publication of the unfinished work in the immediate aftermath of its
author's death. When the novel finally appeared in 1994, it aroused
considerable interest in France. By then Algeria was in the grip of
civil war between a military-led government and Islamist insurgents.
By then too, a number of influential Algerian novelists had given
voice to their sense of connection to Camus as an Algerian writer.[17]

In his *Requiem for a Nun*, Faulkner wrote of 'the long weary
increment since Genesis'.[18] There is an echo of this millennial scale
in Camus' choice of *The First Man* as the title for a work which casts
Jacques Cormery as a figure lost in a long line of settler descendants.
Camus concluded Part One of the novel by juxtaposing 'the first
mornings of the world' and 'the world of the men of his time and its
dreadful and exalted history' (*FM*, 153). He had recognized in
Requiem for a Nun the perspective of a visionary. As Faulkner tells
the history of the fictional Yoknapatawpha County in the prose narrative sections that precede the work's three acts, he writes about
'the ravaged' and 'the ravager' and evokes the waves of settlement
that had seen the Native American population supplanted: 'the dispossessed, dispossessed by those who were dispossessed in turn
because they too were obsolete'.[19] Camus was likewise superimpos-
ing dominated and dominant in his representation of the French
presence in Algeria. Thus those who, with the Prussian annexation
of Alsace and Lorraine in 1871, left eastern France and settled land
in Algeria that had been expropriated by the French after the

quelling of the major insurrection of 1871 led by Sheik Mokrani are cast as 'the persecuted-turned-persecutors' (*les persécutés-persécuteurs*). The category signals a world of moral ambivalence. And yet Jacques Cormery comes to feel the shame of this ambivalence when, having identified instinctively with all victims, he now painfully acknowledges his complicity with the 'executioners' (*FM*, 247). Camus may have heeded his public vow of silence on Algeria after the publication of *Algerian Chronicles* in 1958 but through the pages of *The First Man*, his soul-searching continued.

In the final chapter of Part One of the novel, the language of 'the vast throng of the nameless dead' and 'the night of the years in the land of oblivion' (*FM*, 151–2) again has a Faulknerian ring to it. Both authors were constructing narratives of settler loss. Faulkner describes the arrival in Mississippi of the Huguenot slaver Louis Grenier and the future demise of his household,

> which a hundred years later will have vanished, his name and his blood too, leaving nothing but the name of his plantation and his own fading corrupted legend like a thin layer of the native ephemeral yet inevictable dust on a section of country surrounding a little lost paintless crossroads store.[20]

No less apocalyptic is the perspective in *The First Man*: 'All those generations, all those men come from so many nations . . . had disappeared without a trace . . . An enormous oblivion spread over them' (*FM*, 150).[21]

Camus' premature death made *The First Man* his last work. Yet in a conversation in the summer of 1959 with his old friend the architect Jean de Maisonseul, he suggested that he was only a third of the way through his writing career and that with *The First Man*, he felt he was starting for real.[22]

In his notebooks, Camus was reflecting on his complicated emotional life. He remained on intimate terms with Maria Casares and Catherine Sellers. For the last years of his life, he was also in a relationship with a young Scandinavian woman, Mi. A notebook entry for late April 1959 shows him setting out how after years of attempting to live by conventional morality he had given up:

> Now I wander among the debris, I am without law, torn apart, alone and accepting to be so, resigned to my singularity and my infirmities. And I must reconstruct a truth – after living all my life in a sort of lie (*oc*, IV, 1296).

His protagonist Jacques Cormery is described as being in relationships with four women and confesses to feeling emptiness (*fm*, 234), and isolation forms a recurring theme in Camus' late diary entries: 'I cannot live for a long time with people. I need a bit of solitude, a little piece of eternity' (*oc*, IV, 1303), he concluded. A sombre, brooding tone coloured his reflection on questions to do with attachment and fidelity: 'All my life as soon as someone became attached to me, I did all I could so that the person would step back' (*oc*, IV, 1306). There was lucidity in his attempt to work out his own psychological motivation and he saw the link between his crisis as a writer and emotional neediness: 'Since being in this crisis, in this sort of impotence, I can understand that ignoble desire for possession which when seen in other people has always scandalized me' (*oc*, IV, 1306).

Camus was last in Paris in November 1959. He had lunch there with Catherine Sellers on his 46th birthday and a week later returned to Lourmarin where he was determined to press ahead with *The First Man*. He explained that there was no joy in the writing process, which he defined as 'an effort of daily concentration, of intellectual asceticism' (*oc*, IV, 1301). Reflecting more widely, he revealed that the most exhausting effort in his whole life had been to 'curb my own nature to make it serve my more worthy plans' (*oc*, IV, 1302).

Weeks before he died, he evoked for Mi the frustration this entailed. He complained that being naturally given to pleasure and laughter, he found the near-monastic isolation needed to write unbearable:

> I lash out, I stamp my feet, I snap my jaws and even go as far as grabbing myself by the scruff of the neck and setting myself down in front of the paper. Yesterday, having wasted time for almost half an hour, I shouted insults at myself for five minutes. Then I started behaving and got back into the work with my tail between my legs.[23]

The search for patience was, in Camus' words, the 'only method that suits my horrible anarchy'.

What turned out to be Camus' last public meeting was on 14 December 1959 with a group of international students in Aix-en-Provence, 25 miles from Lourmarin. He fielded a range of questions from his audience, wondering aloud if he really was an intellectual and explaining the scope of his next work (*The First Man*), which, he revealed, was to be about his own life and his century.[24] His wife Francine and their children, Catherine and Jean, joined him at Lourmarin for Christmas and the family saw in the New Year there. Michel and Janine Gallimard and their daughter Anne called with them on the way up from the Mediterranean coast. Together they celebrated Anne's eighteenth birthday. Francine returned to Paris with the twins by train on 2 January. Camus left by car with the Gallimards the following day. They broke the journey and were due back in Paris on the evening of 4 January 1960. Early that afternoon, the car left the road at Villeblevin, north of Sens. Camus was killed instantly. Janine and Anne Gallimard survived and Michel Gallimard died five days later in hospital.

16

A Contested Legacy

To understand historical reality, it is sometimes necessary *not to know the outcome*.

Pierre Vidal-Naquet[1]

As Raymond Aron pointed out, Camus was a writer and not a politician.[2] By his own admission, he was 'not cut out for politics since I am incapable of wanting or accepting the death of the adversary'.[3] His connection with the events of his day could be direct and intense as is shown by his work as a journalist at *Alger-républicain*, *Combat* and *L'Express*. In *Combat* in December 1944 he argued that 'the nations of the world have a common destiny' (*CAC*, 397) and that the industrial growth of one state and the pauperization of another impacted on countries far and wide. He put the global argument anecdotally when he suggested that a slap on the face for someone in Prague could affect the lives of a Ukrainian, a farmer in Texas and a bourgeois from Fontainebleau. Yet paradoxically Camus also showed a more oblique connection with the events of his day. While no stranger to polemic, he came to see in the 1950s that public controversy was sapping the energy he needed to be a writer. Nor did he want to see the autonomy of creative writing compromised by calls to be socially engaged.

If the suggestion in *The First Man* of a 'collective destiny' points to Camus' life and work being increasingly identified with the fortunes specifically of French Algeria, it would be wrong to see the linkage as summing up his life as a writer. In a 1955 preface to the Tunisian Jewish writer Albert Memmi's autobiographical novel *La Statue de sel* (Pillar of Salt), Camus distanced himself from any conflation of nationality and selfhood. The preface throws light on Memmi's marginal situation but also indirectly on Camus. He reconstructs the dilemma facing a writer growing up in colonial Tunisia as a member of the country's minority Jewish population. Memmi lost his religious faith and by attending the French lycée in Tunis discovered a European world that was alienating for this 'son of Africa'.

If in Memmi's self-definition he is irretrievably marginalized (as an African facing European domination and as a Jew living in a Muslim country), Camus saw this tension as delivering the birth of the writer:

> a writer is to be defined first of all by his inability . . . to merge into the anonymity of a race or class. In any case, there is no doubt that for Memmi, this unbelieving Paul-like figure, writing was his road to Damascus (*oc*, III, 1122).

Camus was thus distinguishing between tribal allegiance and a writer's autonomy. In the closing section of his preface, he endorses Memmi's project, arguing that the wrench or *déchirement* which he as a Jew has experienced in turn throws light on the wider contradiction that is lived by the other parties, namely Arabs and French. Camus argues in his conclusion to the Memmi preface that with North Africa now living through a bloody period in its history, 'all of us, the French and the indigenous population of North Africa' must remain conscious of the contradictions and triumph over them by living them fully. Camus thus read Memmi's trajectory sympathetically. And indeed his insistence on the inability of the writer to embrace the 'anonymity of a class or a tribe' suggests an impatience with the typecasting that he himself came to experience.

The strain of independent-mindedness ran deep in Camus. An early article entitled 'Considérations inactuelles' (Considerations Irrelevant to the Present Day) carried echoes of Nietzsche's *Unzeitgemäss*. Camus used the article, published under the pseudonym Nero in *Le Soir républicain* on 6 November 1939, to define what he meant by independence. It was, he said, a rare virtue, to be practised by the individual first in relation to himself. It made possible the shedding of one's own prejudices and this in turn fed into rejection of the wider social prejudices which led to human destructiveness. Conscious that independence was 'his only treasure', the individual had to defend it 'against every attempt at domestication or enslavement' (*oc*, I, 771).

Literature had helped shape this outlook of detachment. *Don Quixote* deeply influenced Camus (as did Tolstoy's *War and Peace* and Pascal's *Pensées*). In an article on Cervantes published in *Le Monde libertaire* on 12 November 1955 to mark the 350th anniversary of publication of Part One of *Don Quixote*, he confessed to feeling drawn to a novelistic hero whose lifestyle embodied a resistance to actuality. Five times in the short article, he uses the term *inactualité* (irrelevance to the present day), which he also paraphrases as the stubborn refusal of the realities of the century (*oc*, III, 979–81).

This ambiguous connection with the age was something he shared with René Char. The poet had suggested to Camus in late 1953 that with French intellectual life a 'mass grave', they had to accept being 'these Don Quixotes' who, though shipwrecked, press on even if the destination is unclear.[4] There is an element of self-portrait in a late manuscript note where Camus describes Char as being anchored to his age and yet standing alone surrounded by 'stagnant waters and prattlers'. Camus noted with approval the line in Char's brief poem 'Contrevenir' (Contravening): 'Obey your swine who exist. I submit to my gods who do not exist. We remain people of inclemency.'[5]

If Char's 'inclemency' suggested a stubborn turning away from the present, Camus, writing in a similar vein, posed the question: 'What can the artist do in today's world?' (*oc*, III, 453–4) in the closing section of *Actuelles II* in 1953. He rejected both any retreat into the ivory tower and the uncompromising choice of 'the social church'. He returned to the question of the artist and his times in a short reflection in *L'Express* on 20 December 1955. Taking as his point of departure the story of the Hungarian musician Tibot Harsanyi, who for years had tried to obtain French citizenship, Camus describes the artist as a figure who is pressed on two sides: ignored by bourgeois society, he is also harassed by the 'so-called revolutionary society' which lays claim to his allegiance (*oc*, III, 1063). In the case of Harsanyi, Camus protested, a civil servant had given as the grounds for refusal of French nationality the fact that he 'exercises a socially useless profession' (*oc*, III, 1062).

In some journal notes of 1956, Camus drew on Tolstoy's distinction between two categories of literature: political literature, which had the importance of mirroring what was transient in society; and a literature which connected with the 'eternal preoccupations shared by the whole of humanity' (*oc*, IV, 1249). The attrition caused by the Cold War and the crisis in Algeria accounted for Camus' longing in the 1950s to get beyond 'political literature'. Thus while Sartre and others called for literature to be socially committed, Camus worked to assert the writer's autonomy. Annie Cohen-Solal contrasts the evolution in the careers of both writers, pointing out that whereas Sartre became increasingly committed politically with the crisis in Algeria, Camus, having been engaged in the Second World War, had come to adopt 'that strangely agnostic position in which the political became blurred and ethical questions came to the fore'.[6]

The shock of the news of Camus' death on 4 January 1960 was intense. Writing in *France Observateur* on 7 January 1960, Sartre asserted that their being fallen out had been just another

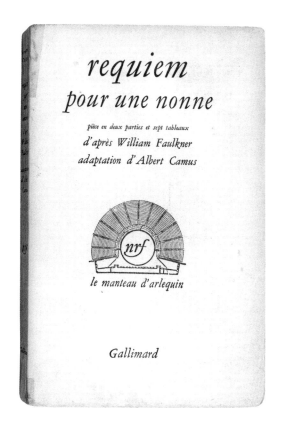

requiem
pour une nonne

pièce en deux parties et sept tableaux
d'après William Faulkner
adaptation d'Albert Camus

nrf

le manteau d'arlequin

Gallimard

Front cover
of the *Hommage
à Albert Camus*,
published by
*La Nouvelle
Revue française*,
March 1960.

way of living together 'in the little narrow world that is given
to us'. He paid tribute to his deceased rival as someone 'who
was changing with the world as were the rest of us'.[7] Even if
decorum required a show of decency in a memorial tribute,
the contrast with Sartre's calculated act of humiliation directed
against Camus in August 1952 was stark. Sartre now positioned
Camus in an illustrious line of French moralists: 'at the heart
of our time and era, he reaffirmed, against the Machiavellians
and the golden calf of realism, the existence of the moral
dimension'.[8]

In March 1960, the *Nouvelle Revue française* published a collective memorial tribute, *Hommage à Albert Camus*. Introducing the special issue, Maurice Blanchot chose a letter written by the dying Turgenev to Tolstoy to convey something of his own emotion: 'I am writing to you to say how happy I was to be your contemporary.'[9] He went on to reflect that for Camus personally, the publication of his works had been experienced as a form of malaise, as though in their finished form and given the celebrity they brought, the works had immobilized their author. For Blanchot, Camus' writing retained its mystery beyond the reputation which the published work had acquired. William Faulkner, turning attention away from Camus' premature death, reflected that the issue was not to do with the number of years of life nor the quantity of work Camus produced:

> When the door shut for him, he had already written on this side of it that which every artist who also carries through life with him that one same foreknowledge and hatred of death, is hoping to do: *I was here.*[10]

For many, mourning Camus was inextricably tied up with the ongoing war in Algeria. In Algiers Mouloud Feraoun saw the news of his death as another element in the country's tragedy.[11] In the case of Jules Roy, Camus' sudden death shaped his friend's writing in a very concrete way. Roy wrote *La Guerre d'Algérie* (The Algerian War) hurriedly in July–August 1960. The book contained 'plastic explosive', to use Roy's metaphor, since it urged the French to understand the blunt reality of French military repression in the country and to see the link between that and FLN violence. Dedicating the work to Camus' memory, Roy described in his introduction how his identification with the deceased author had literally taken him back to Algeria to investigate the situation, in deference to Camus' achievement in the making of *Algerian*

Chronicles. Roy described himself as being like Camus, torn between the need to see justice for the country's Muslim population and his connection with the European Algerians.[12]

In mourning his friend, Roy also saw himself as performing an act of witness, speaking about Algeria even if this meant investigating the motivations of the enemies of French Algeria.[13] In an imagined conversation with the dead author, Roy reported on passing through Mondovi (Camus' birthplace near Bône/Annaba), which now bore the signs of the military conflict.[14]

Algeria also featured in the NRF tribute to Camus in March 1960, an article by Robert Mallet reconstructing a conversation in December 1958 when Mallet suggested that the author of *Algerian Chronicles* might be able to help in the conflict. Camus set out his reasons for not intervening:

> Nationalists on both sides are suspicious of me. To one side, I am not . . . patriotic enough. To the other, I am too patriotic. I don't love Algeria in the way that someone in the military or a colonialist might do. But can I love it other than as a Frenchman? What too many Arabs don't understand is that I love it as a Frenchman who loves the Arabs and who wants them to feel at home in their own country in Algeria without feeling himself to be an outsider there.[15]

Looking back on Camus' strained connection with Algeria in the last years of his life, Mohammed Dib insisted in a 1972 interview that he was 'the brother who exiled himself following a misunderstanding, one of those expressions of mood which are always somewhat spectacular in people from the shores of the Mediterranean'.[16] It was, Dib conceded, a painful misunderstanding but one that reflected an Algerian culture of 'exaggeration . . . and theatricality'. For him, the connection with Camus remained fundamentally fraternal.

Likewise, the Francophone Algerian writer Assia Djebar has drawn the loss of Camus into the nation's mourning for those of its writers who died in the second half of the twentieth century and particularly in the years of the War of Independence and the Algerian Civil War of the 1990s. In particular Djebar sees in the Camus who called for a civilian truce in January 1956 a moving figure 'at the centre of the arena'; he was articulating, she writes, 'words of helplessness that are not entirely impotent, those words

Camus' grave in Lourmarin in the Vaucluse, southeast France.

of a suffering which hopes one last time'.[17] Djebar wonders who in the 1990s, at the time of Algeria's Civil War, might follow Camus' lead. The violence of that conflict prompts Salim Bachi to reflect that it has led to a better appreciation of the constraints facing Camus in the late 1950s when, with family still living in Algiers, he was reluctant to intervene further, knowing that such a move could leave them vulnerable.[18]

Yet it would be wrong to see in these conciliatory voices from postcolonial Algeria proof that Camus' work has been received uncritically in a postcolonial age. The historian Benjamin Stora has noted that when French President François Hollande addressed the Algerian parliament in December 2012, his mention of Albert Camus was received in silence by the assembled parliamentarians. Work was needed, Stora argues, to 'add Camus to that history', Stora calling for the inclusion rather than the subtraction of distinctive cultural memories in respect of the history of twentieth-century Algeria.[19]

Back in 1961, Pierre Nora had argued that Camus' legacy was no less contentious than the French presence itself.[20] If Nora's provocative coupling of writer and colonial rule was intentionally polemical (he was actively campaigning for an end to colonial rule when his *Les Français d'Algérie* appeared in March 1961), it contributed towards an attitude of suspicion in relation to Camus. In the Anglophone world Conor Cruise O'Brien's study of 1970 would draw on this view of a writer seen as an apologist for French colonial rule. Reading Camus against the background of the colonial legacy continues to feature in more recent studies of the author in the field of postcolonial criticism.[21] But as Camus' contemporary Mouloud Mammeri, a Kabyle writer, has pointed out, for someone of Camus' class and background (he was as we have seen a 'petit blanc', a working-class French Algerian), the cultural attitudes he reflected were unexceptional and while he worked to reach intellectually and ideologically beyond the world of colonial Algiers, the specificities of class and race remained historically significant determinants.[22]

Camus' legacy nevertheless extends beyond the conflicted history of Franco–Algerian relations and the postcolonial evaluation of colonial culture. The emergence from the Cold War and the collapse of the former Soviet Union provided an additional significant framework within which his work came to be keenly read. Jean Daniel has observed that after Camus' death, his work was appropriated by the bourgeoisie, leading to the Left dismissing his so-called Red Cross morality. In an interview with Jean-Claude Brisville in 1959, Camus agreed that admiration for a writer may be based on misunderstanding and confessed to feeling irritated by talk of his being on the side of 'honesty', 'conscience' and 'humanity' (*oc*, IV, 614). The moralized tone of works such as *Letters to a German Friend* and *The Plague* had contributed to that reputation. But in 1954, working on a preface for Konrad Bieber's study *L'Allemagne vue par les écrivains de la Résistance française* (Germany as Seen by Writers of the French Resistance), Camus rejected Bieber's portrait of him as 'a man of justice': 'I am a man without justice but one who is tormented by that infirmity, that's all' (*oc*, III, 937).

Reappraising Camus' work as a journalist at *Combat*, the former Communist Edgar Morin came to recognize that Camus

> had the merit of shaking off early the euphoria of the Left and even in a sense of taking refuge in the retreat of solitary consciousness. But at the time, I renounced the noble soul (*belle âme*) in him and each time he made a moral pronouncement I only ever saw it as a retreat into subjectivity, a defeat, even a pose that was too easy, in short as an abandonment of the constraints which revolutionary combat implies.[23]

Morin's revised, conciliatory view of Camus forms part of a wider return to an author who had been rejected by many on the Left in France. As Jean Daniel has noted, Camus' influence in central and Eastern Europe was real and significant, as illustrated by the endorsements of such figures as Hannah Arendt, Alexander Solzhenitsyn, Milan Kundera and the Polish poet Czestław Miłosz.[24] Accepting the Nobel Prize in 1970, Solzhenitsyn commented that, within the periodic 'heated, angry and exquisite debates as to whether art and the artist . . . should be for ever mindful of their duty towards society', Camus' Nobel speech reflected Solzhenitsyn's own conclusions.

Asked in a late interview about how he came to write, Camus reflected: 'I wanted to be a writer from about the age of seventeen. At the same time, I knew in an obscure sort of way that I would be one' (*oc*, IV, 610–11). His experience of the career of writer was like that of the painter Jonas in *Exile and the Kingdom*, torn between solidarity and solitude. Celebrity and controversy came Camus' way in equal measure. He was accused of disloyalty by colonialists when he advocated social and economic reform in Algeria in 1939; was an isolated voice when protesting in the immediate aftermath of Hiroshima; was caricatured by Sartre in 1952 as the Saint Vincent de Paul of sanctimoniousness when he opposed the politics of the Soviet Union; branded disloyal to the European side by speaking out against the killing in Paris on Bastille Day 1953 of North African protestors; labelled a traitor by French Algerian loyalists when he campaigned for a civilian truce in January 1956; and cast as an apologist for French military repression in the Algerian War. He was repeatedly typecast as standing above the fray; as aligning himself with a humanist morality which in a broader context Merleau-Ponty dismissed as being 'celestial and intransigent'; or as 'the Master of the Absolute', in Jean Sénac's stinging rebuke.[25] The litany of rejections is long and testifies to the controversy he attracted.

Just as in his lifetime he felt estranged from colonial Algeria's 'two nationalisms', as we saw earlier in this chapter, so in death Camus' legacy has been the subject of appropriation and misrepresentation. Those nostalgic for the days of empire wish to lay exclusive claim to his memory and work, while in postcolonial readings of his corpus, some continue to see him as an embodiment of colonialist reaction.

Camus did not aspire to a moral monopoly. He accurately conceded that 'this book is . . . the story of a failure' (*oc*, IV, 303) in reference to his *Algerian Chronicles*, which can indeed be read as charting the political and social impasse that colonial Algeria had reached. Edward Said would write of the 'negative vitality' to be found in Camus' works, where, he argues, 'the tragic human seriousness of the colonial effort achieves its last great clarification before ruin overtakes it. They express a waste and sadness we have still not completely understood or recovered from.'[26]

Camus' was indeed a 'critical life' lived in the critical times that were the early to middle decades of twentieth-century Algeria and France. In a diary entry of 1946 he wrote that he preferred committed people to committed literature:

> Courage in one's life and talent in one's works, that's not bad at all. And then the writer is engaged when he wishes. His merit lies in this movement and fluctuation. And if engagement should become a law, a profession or a form of tyranny, where's the merit in that?[27]

The no-nonsense prescription captures the independent-mindedness of an author who, while reaching a global audience, privately doubted his ability to write and who frequently found the isolation needed for textual composition alienating. He lived intensely the dilemmas confronting the writer in an age of conflict. In the final lines of *Actuelles II* in 1953, Camus called on the artist to avoid internalizing the negative view of the writer as a figure disconnected from society. He went on to say that a society without culture and without 'the relative freedom this supposes' is a jungle. But in valuing the role of the artist, he also proposed a principle of equalization whereby the artist is 'neither higher nor lower than all those who work and struggle' (*oc*, III, 455).

References

Introduction: 'Who is Camus?'

1 Louis Germain, letter to Camus, 30 April 1959, *FM*, 258.
2 See Pierre-Louis Rey's editorial introduction to Camus' *L'Été*
  (Summer) and in particular *OC*, III, 1331. See also Herbert R.
  Lottman, *Albert Camus: A Biography* [1979] (Corte Madera, CA, 1997),
  p. 554.
3 Jean-Paul Sartre in *France Observateur* (7 January 1960); reproduced
  in Sartre, *Situations*, IV (Paris, 1964), p. 128.
4 See Renaud de Rochebrune and Benjamin Stora, *La Guerre d'Algérie
  vue par les Algériens* (Paris, 2011), pp. 55–63.
5 See John Talbott, 'French Public Opinion and the Algerian War:
  A Research Note', *French Historical Studies*, IX/2 (1975), pp. 354–61
  (p. 358); cited in Daniel Just, *Literature, Ethics, and Decolonization in
  Postwar France: The Politics of Disengagement* (Cambridge, 2015), p. 9.
6 Azzedine Haddour notes the massive scale of expropriation of native
  Berber land with the suppression of the uprising in A. Haddour,
  'Bread and Wine: Bourdieu's Photography of Colonial Algeria',
  Sociological Review, LVII/3 (August 2009), pp. 385–405 (p. 395).
7 Quoted in Benjamin Stora and Jean-Baptiste Péretié, *Camus brûlant*
  (Paris, 2013), p. 102.
8 See Albert Camus, *L'Été*, *OC*, III, 606.
9 Isaiah Berlin, quoted in Eric Hobsbawm, *Age of Extremes: The Short
  Twentieth Century, 1914–1991* (London, 1995), p. 1.
10 Peter Dunwoodie, 'Negotiation or Confrontation? Camus, Memory
  and the Colonial Chronotope', in *Albert Camus in the 21st Century:
  A Reassessment of his Thinking at the Dawn of the New Millennium*,

ed. Christine Margerrison, Mark Orme and Lissa Lincoln (Amsterdam, 2008), pp. 45–60 (p. 60).

1 Literacy, or 'the Regular Rows of the Lines'

1 *FM*, 194.
2 See Daniel Lefeuvre, 'Les pieds-noirs', in *La Guerre d'Algérie: 1954–2004, la fin de l'amnésie*, ed. Mohammed Harbi and Benjamin Stora (Paris, 2004), pp. 267–86 (p. 272). See also Benjamin Stora, *La Guerre d'Algérie (1954–1962)* (Paris, 2004), p. 14.
3 Annie Cohen-Solal, *Sartre, 1905–1980* (Paris, 1985), p. 433.
4 Albert Camus and Jean Grenier, *Correspondance, 1932–1960*, ed. Marguerite Dobrenn (Paris, 1981), pp. 80–81.
5 See Pierre-Louis Rey's excellent chronology of Camus' life, 'Chronologie', *oc*, I, lxix–xcviii (pp. lxx–lxxi).
6 Max-Pol Fouchet, *Un jour, je m'en souviens* (Paris, 1968), pp. 11–12.
7 Quoted in Camus and Grenier, *Correspondance*, p. 77.
8 Benjamin Stora and Jean-Baptiste Péretié, *Camus brûlant* (Paris, 2013), p. 68.
9 Ibid., p. 69.

2 'True Love . . . Awkward Pages'

1 Information provided by Louis Guilloux. See Albert Camus and Louis Guilloux, *Correspondance: 1945–1959*, ed. Agnès Spiquel-Courdille (Paris, 2013), p. 201.
2 Jean Grenier, 'Les Iles Fortunées' (The Fortunate Isles), cited by Toby Garfitt, 'Situating Camus: The Formative Influences', in *The Cambridge Companion to Camus*, ed. Edward J. Hughes (Cambridge, 2007), p. 30.
3 Camus, 'Préface', Jean Grenier, *Les Iles* [1959] (Paris, 2012), p. 10.
4 Ibid.
5 Ibid., p. 13.
6 Ibid., p. 14.
7 See Olivier Todd, *Albert Camus: une vie* (Paris, 1996), p. 51.

8 Dante, *Paradise*, I. 34, quoted in J. Grenier, 'Il me serait impossible
. . .', in *Hommage à Albert Camus 1913–1960, Nouvelle Revue française*,
LXXXVII (March 1960), p. 409.

9 Max-Pol Fouchet, *Un jour, je m'en souviens* (Paris, 1968), pp. 16–17.

10 See Albert Camus and Jean Grenier, *Correspondance, 1932–1960*, ed.
Marguerite Dobrenn (Paris, 1981), pp. 15, 237.

11 This text forms part of the appended material to *L'Envers et l'Endroit*
and is reproduced in *OC*, I, 75–86.

12 Camus, *Carnets*, *OC*, II, 795. Emphasis in the original.

13 *OC*, II, 830; quoted in Sophie Doudet, Marcelle Mahasela, Pierre-Louis
Rey, Agnès Spiquel and Maurice Weyembergh, *Albert Camus: Citoyen
du monde* (Paris, 2013), p. 167.

3 'This Algiers Happiness'

1 Max-Paul Fouchet, *Un jour, je m'en souviens* (Paris, 1968), pp. 24–5.

2 Henry de Montherlant, *Il y a encore des paradis: Images d'Alger
1928–1931* (Algiers, 1935), p. 23.

3 For an image of the original manuscript page, see Sophie Doudet,
Marcelle Mahasela, Pierre-Louis Rey, Agnès Spiquel and Maurice
Weyembergh, *Albert Camus: Citoyen du monde* (Paris, 2013), p. 182.

4 Simone de Beauvoir, *La Force des choses* (Paris, 1963), p. 180.

5 The essay would feature in the collection *L'Été*, which was published
in 1954.

6 David Prochaska notes that between the turn of the twentieth century
and the outbreak of war in 1914, a fusion leading to the formation of
an identifiably European settler community had taken place. See
Prochaska, *Making Algeria French: Colonialism in Bône, 1870–1920*
(Cambridge, 1990), p. 25.

4 All Work and No Play

1 Roger Grenier, ed., *Album Camus* (Paris, 1982), p. 182.

5 A Beautiful Profession

1 Christiane Achour, *Un Etranger si familier: Lecture du récit d'Albert Camus* (Algiers, 1984), p. 44.

2 See Pierre-Louis Rey, 'Chronologie', *oc*, i, lxxvi.

3 Camus' comment featured in the journal *Caliban*, LIV (August 1951); cited in editorial note, Albert Camus and Louis Guilloux, *Correspondance, 1945–1959*, ed. Agnès Spiquel-Courdille (Paris, 2013), p. 159.

4 Jacqueline Lévi-Valensi and André Abbou, eds, *Fragments d'un combat 1938–1940: Alger Républicain/Le Soir Républicain* (Paris, 1978), p. 45.

5 Louis Guilloux, *La Maison du peuple suivi de Compagnons* (Paris, 1953), p. 57.

6 See Lévi-Valensi and Abbou, eds, *Fragments d'un combat*, p. 542.

7 Cited in Michel Onfray, *L'Ordre libertaire: La vie philosophique d'Albert Camus* (Paris, 2012), p. 29.

8 See Patrick McCarthy, *Camus* (New York, 1982), p. 50.

9 Jean Grenier, 'Ils ont faim' (They are hungry), *Nouvelle Revue française*, CCXCI (1 December 1937), p. 1040.

10 The term 'actuelles' is difficult to translate succinctly. The sense is of matters that are current and of interest. See Camus, *Resistance, Rebellion, and Death*, trans. Justin O'Brien (London, 1961), translator's note, p. vii.

11 Achour, *Un Etranger si familier*, p. 46.

12 Julian Jackson, *The Popular Front in France: Defending Democracy, 1934–1938* (Cambridge, 1988), p. 156.

13 See McCarthy, *Camus*, p. 50.

14 Mouloud Feraoun, 'Le Dernier Message', *Preuves* (April 1960), reproduced in Feraoun, *L'Anniversaire* (Paris, 1972), pp. 45–52 (p. 49).

6 A Tale of Two Outsiders

1 Quoted in Sophie Doudet, Marcelle Mahasela, Pierre-Louis Rey, Agnès Spiquel and Maurice Weyembergh, *Albert Camus: Citoyen du monde* (Paris, 2013), p. 122.

2 Quoted in Olivier Todd, *Albert Camus: une vie* (Paris, 1996), p. 221.

3 Camus, *The Outsider*, trans. Sandra Smith (London, 2012), p. 3.

4 Albert Camus and Jean Grenier, *Correspondance, 1932–1960*, ed. Marguerite Dobrenn (Paris, 1981), p. 29.

5 *OC*, IV, 1384, editorial note by M. Weyembergh.

6 See Dominique Rabaté, 'Roman', in *Dictionnaire Albert Camus*, ed. Jeanyves Guérin (Paris, 2009), p. 803.

7 Jean-Paul Sartre, 'Explication de "L'Etranger"', *Situations*, I [1947] (Paris, 1964), pp. 99–121 (p. 99).

8 Ibid., p. 120.

9 See André Abbou's introduction to the novel, *OC*, I, 1252. Abbou cites the case of the Bollota Affair, for example, as reported in *La Dépêche algérienne* on 6 July 1939.

10 See Abbou's editorial note, *OC*, I, 1259.

11 Derrida's letter of 27 April 1961 is reproduced in Pierre Nora, *Les Français d'Algérie* (Paris, 2012), pp. 271–99.

12 Quoted in Conor Cruise O'Brien, *Camus* [1970] (London, 1982), p. 25.

13 Nora, *Les Français d'Algérie*, p. 209.

14 Ibid.

15 Edward Said, *Culture and Imperialism* (London, 1994), p. 224.

16 Sartre, *Situations*, I, p. 102.

7 'All Man's Misery . . .'

1 Julian Jackson, *France: The Dark Years, 1940–1944* (Oxford, 2001), p. 120.

2 See Antony Beevor and Artemis Cooper, *Paris after the Liberation: 1944–1949* (London, 1995), p. 15.

3 Quoted in Olivier Todd, *Albert Camus: une vie* (Paris, 1996), p. 256.

4 Quoted ibid., p. 221.

5 Quoted in Jean Daniel, *Avec Camus: Comment résister à l'air du temps* (Paris, 2006), p. 42.

6 André Kaspi, *Les Juifs pendant l'Occupation* (Paris, 1991); quoted in Todd, *Albert Camus: une vie*, p. 265.

7 Albert Camus and Jean Grenier, *Correspondance, 1932–1960*, ed. Marguerite Dobrenn (Paris, 1981), p. 59.

8 Camus, *The Plague*, trans. Robin Buss (London, 2002), p. 5.

9 Camus and Grenier, *Correspondance*, pp. 67, 69.

10 Ibid., p. 88.

11 Ibid., p. 89.

12 Albert Camus and Francis Ponge, *Correspondance, 1941–1957*, ed. Jean-Marie Gleize (Paris, 2013), pp. 73–4.

13 Quoted in Herbert R. Lottman, *Albert Camus: A Biography* [1979] (Corte Madera, CA, 1997), p. 288.

14 Camus and Grenier, *Correspondance*, p. 85.

15 Ibid., p. 89.

16 Ibid., p. 87.

17 Maria Casarès, *Résidente privilégiée* (Paris, 1980), p. 232.

18 Quoted in James Kirkup's obituary for Maria Casares, *The Guardian* (26 November 1996).

19 See David H. Walker's editorial note, *OC*, I, 1339, n. 5.

20 Testimony of Béatrix Dussane, teacher and friend of Casares, reproduced in Lottman, *Albert Camus*, p. 336.

21 *Combat clandestin*, LVIII (July 1944); quoted in *CAC*, 134.

22 Camus' letter to Ponge, 30 August 1943. See Camus and Ponge, *Correspondance*, p. 73.

23 Camus, *The Plague*, p. 223; translation slightly modified.

24 *OC*, II, 1303, note 11.

25 Jacques Roubaud, *Poésie* (Paris, 1967). The references are taken from Emmanuelle Tabet's 'Pascal' entry in *Le Dictionnaire Albert Camus*, ed. Jeanyves Guérin (Paris, 2009), p. 649.

26 The French original in Pascal reads: 'tout le malheur des hommes vient d'une seule chose, qui est de ne savoir pas demeurer en repos dans une chambre', B. Pascal, *Pensées*, ed. Louis Lafuma (Paris, 1962), p. 77; Albert Camus and Louis Guilloux, *Correspondance, 1945–1959*, ed. Agnès Spiquel-Courdille (Paris, 2013), p. 34.

8 *Combat* and the Narrative of Liberation

1 From a piece by Camus on the role of the journalist intended for publication in *Le Soir républicain* (25 November 1939) and censored. Article reproduced with an introduction by Macha Séry, *Le Monde* (18 March 2012).

2 Jeanyves Guérin, '*Combat*', in *Dictionnaire Albert Camus*, ed. J. Guérin (Paris, 2009), p. 164.

3 François Mauriac, 'Le Mépris de la charité', *Le Figaro* (7–8 January 1945), quoted in *CAC*, 433, editorial note 1.

4 See *Albert Camus contre la peine de mort*, ed. Eve Morisi and with preface by Robert Badinter (Paris, 2011), pp. 18–19.

5 Simone de Beauvoir, *La Force des choses* (Paris, 1963), p. 43.

6 The journalist Wladimir d'Ormesson had reported along these lines in *Le Figaro* (8 March 1945). See editorial note 1, *CAC*, 500.

7 See Lévi-Valensi's editorial note 2, *OC*, II, 1300.

8 Patrick McCarthy, *Camus* (New York, 1982), p. 204.

9 See the historian Michel Winock's views quoted by Guérin, '*Combat*', p. 165.

10 For a brief period in the spring of 1947, Camus stepped in to run *Combat* when Pascal Pia resigned, having switched his political allegiance to De Gaulle.

11 See J. Guérin, 'Ni victimes ni bourreaux', in *Dictionnaire Albert Camus*, pp. 610–13.

12 See Herbert R. Lottman, *Albert Camus: A Biography* [1979] (Corte Madera, CA, 1997), chapter 29, 'New York', pp. 397–417.

13 Albert Camus and Louis Guilloux, *Correspondance, 1945–1959*, ed. Agnès Spiquel-Courdille (Paris, 2013), p. 48.

14 Ibid., pp. 51–2.

15 Ibid., p. 88.

16 Ibid.

17 Ibid., p. 154.

9 'A Catastrophe Slow to Happen'

1 The first issue of *Les Temps modernes* appeared on 15 October 1945.

2 Merleau-Ponty's review article 'Le Yogi et le prolétaire', first published in *Les Temps modernes* in January 1947, was reproduced in his *Humanisme et terreur: Essai sur le problème communiste* (Paris, 1947).

3 Arthur Koestler, *The Yogi and the Commissar and other Essays* [1945] (London, 1947), p. 9.

4 Ibid., p. 12.

5 Merleau-Ponty, *Humanisme et terreur*, p. 186.

6 Ibid., p. 188.

7 Jean-Paul Sartre, *Situations*, IV (Paris, 1964), pp. 215–16.

8 Jean-Paul Sartre, *Situations*, X (Paris, 1976), p. 196.

9 See Annie Cohen-Solal, *Sartre, 1905–1980* (Paris, 1985), p. 433.

10 Simone de Beauvoir, *La Force des choses* (Paris, 1963), p. 215.

11 E. Morin writing in *Autocritique* (Paris, 1959), quoted by Maurice Weyemberg and Raymond Gay-Crosier in their editorial presentation of *L'Homme révolté*, *OC*, III, 1221.

12 See Weyemberg and Gay-Crosier, editorial presentation, *OC*, III, 1221–2.

13 See Steven Ungar, '1945, 15 October: Rebellion or Revolution?', in *A New History of French Literature*, ed. Denis Hollier (Cambridge, MA, 1994), pp. 972–7.

14 Albert Camus and René Char, *Correspondance, 1946–1959*, ed. Franck Planeille (Paris, 2007), p. 49. Italics in the original.

15 Ibid., p. 63.

16 Ibid., p. 68.

17 Ibid., p. 73.

18 Ibid., pp. 79–80.

19 See the journal *Arts* (12 October 1951).

20 Sartre, *Situations*, IV, pp. 91–3.

21 Ibid., p. 98; emphasis in the original.

22 Ibid., p. 108.

23 Ibid., p. 105.

24 Ibid., p. 115.

25 Ibid., p. 118.

26 Ibid., p. 121.

27 Raymond Aron, *L'Opium des intellectuels* (Paris, 1955), p. 68.

28 Ibid., p. 65.

29 Ibid., pp. 62–4.

30 Camus and Char, *Correspondance*, p. 56.

31 Letter of 5 September 1952, quoted in Olivier Todd, *Albert Camus: une vie* (Paris, 1996), p. 573.

32 Bernard-Henri Lévy, *Le Siècle de Sartre* (Paris, 2000), p. 414.

33 Albert Camus and Louis Guilloux, *Correspondance, 1945–1959*, ed. Agnès Spiquel-Courdille (Paris, 2013), p. 131.

10 Wars of Words Continued

1 Albert Camus and Louis Guilloux, *Correspondance, 1945–1959*, ed. Agnès Spiquel-Courdille (Paris, 2013), p. 27.
2 Ibid., p. 154.
3 Jean Daniel, *Avec Camus: Comment résister à l'air du temps* (Paris, 2006), p. 27.
4 Jean Daniel, *Le Nouvel Observateur* (25 September 2013).
5 Camus and Guilloux, *Correspondance*, pp. 165–6.
6 Ibid., p. 171.
7 See ibid., pp. 174–5.
8 Ibid., pp. 176–9.
9 Camus protested against this development in two articles published in *L'Express*. See 'Démocrates, couchez-vous!' (Democrats, lie down!) (18 November 1955; *oc*, III, 1046–8) and 'Les Bonnes Leçons' (The Right Lessons) (9 December 1955; *oc*, III, 1056–8).

11 Beyond Polemic: 'From Now On, Creation'

1 1949 notebook entry by Camus, *oc*, IV, 1074.
2 Paul Ricœur, *La Critique et la conviction: entretien avec François Azouvi et Marc de Launay* (Paris, 2013), p. 46.
3 The publisher was Mazenod.
4 J.-P. Morel, 'Herman Melville', in *Dictionnaire Albert Camus*, ed. Jeanyves Guérin (Paris, 2009), p. 526.
5 See Herbert R. Lottman, *Albert Camus: A Biography* [1979] (Corte Madera, CA, 1997), p. 551.
6 See Pierre Grouix, '*Actuelles II*', in *Dictionnaire Albert Camus*, p. 21. An earlier diary entry of late 1951 again shows Camus wanting to 'suppress . . . polemic totally' and to embrace 'Creation' and 'affirmation' (*oc*, IV, 1121).
7 See Patrick McCarthy, *Camus* (New York, 1982), p. 306.
8 See François Malye and Benjamin Stora, *François Mitterrand et la guerre d'Algérie* (Paris, 2012), p. 253.
9 See Pierre-Louis Rey, 'Chronologie', *oc*, I, xciii.
10 Mohamed Lebjaoui, *Vérités sur la révolution algérienne* (Paris, 1970), p. 40.

11 See David Carroll, *Albert Camus the Algerian: Colonialism, Terrorism, Justice* (New York, 2007), p. 224, n. 20.

12 See Lottman, *Albert Camus*, pp. 671–2.

13 Ibid., p. 585.

12 Staging Confession

1 Quoted in Pierre-Louis Rey, 'Chronologie', *oc*, I, xcii.

2 M. Blanchot, 'La Confession dédaigneuse', *Nouvelle Revue française*, XLVIII (December 1956), pp. 1050–56.

3 Quoted by Gilles Philippe in his editorial note, *oc*, III, 1365.

4 Jean-Paul Sartre, *Situations*, IV (Paris, 1964), p. 97.

5 Ibid., pp. 99, 110.

6 See David H. Walker's introduction to the play, *oc*, III, 1387–97 (p. 1388).

7 Ibid., *oc*, III, 1390–91.

8 Herbert R. Lottman, *Albert Camus: A Biography* [1979] (Corte Madera, CA, 1997), p. 617–18.

9 Letter of September 1956, in Albert Camus and René Char, *Correspondance 1946–1959*, ed. Franck Planeille (Paris, 2007), p. 151.

10 Quoted in Lottman, *Albert Camus*, p. 618.

11 See Walker's introduction to the play, *oc*, III, 1397.

13 Stockholm and the Backdrop to Fame

1 Albert Camus and René Char, *Correspondance, 1946–1959*, ed. Franck Planeille (Paris, 2007), p. 165.

2 Ibid., pp. 206–7.

3 See Nathalie Froloff, 'Prix Nobel', in *Dictionnaire Albert Camus*, ed. Jeanyves Guérin (Paris, 2009), p. 614.

4 The title of the collective volume was *Réflexions sur la peine capitale* (Reflections on the Death Penalty). It also contained an introduction and an essay by Jean Bloch-Michel and was published in Paris by Calmann-Lévy.

5 Assia Djebar, *Le Blanc de l'Algérie* (Paris, 1995), pp. 117–18.

6   See 'Lettre de Jacques Derrida', in Pierre Nora, *Les Français d'Algérie* (Paris, 2012), p. 293.

7   Benjamin Stora, *Histoire de la guerre d'Algérie (1954–1962)* (Paris, 2004), p. 31.

8   See Pierre Vidal-Naquet, *L'Affaire Audin (1957–1978)* (Paris, 1958/1989).

9   Henri Alleg, *La Question* [1958–61] (Paris, 2004), p. 112. The capitalization is in the original.

10   Stora, *Histoire de la guerre d'Algérie*, p. 27.

11   Ibid., p. 31.

12   Tillion's work appeared in *Preuves*, LXXXVII (May 1958) and later in book form in *Les Ennemis complémentaires* (Paris, 1960). Tillion set this out in her review of Pierre Nora's *Les Français d'Algérie* in *L'Express*, 18 March 1961, reproduced in Nora, *Les Français d'Algérie*, pp. 317–27.

13   G. Tillion, *France and Algeria: Complementary Enemies*, trans. Richard Howard (New York, 1961), pp. 3–4.

14   *Simoun*, XXXI (July 1960); quoted in Peter Hallward, *Absolutely Postcolonial: Writing between the Singular and the Specific* (Manchester, 2002), p. 194.

15   Jean Sénac, *Pour une terre possible . . . Poèmes et autres textes inédits* (Paris, 1999), p. 191.

16   Ibid.

17   Ibid., p. 195.

18   Tillion, *France and Algeria*, p. 3.

19   See Daniel Lefeuvre, 'Les pieds-noirs', in *La Guerre d'Algérie, 1954–2004: la fin de l'amnésie*, ed. Mohammed Harbi and Benjamin Stora (Paris, 2004), pp. 267–86 (p. 278).

20   Tillion, *France and Algeria*, pp. 4–5.

14   1958

1   Quoted by Camus in a diary entry of 1939 (*OC*, II, 881).

2   Albert Camus and Jean Grenier, *Correspondance, 1932–1960*, ed. Marguerite Dobrenn (Paris, 1981), p. 216.

3   See André Abbou, *Albert Camus entre les lignes: Adieu à la littérature ou fausse sortie? 1955–1959* (Biarritz, 2009), p. 174.

4   'Je vous ai compris' suivi de 'L'Algérie n'est pas la France' et de 'Le Droit à l'insoumission' (Paris, 2011), pp. 13–14.

5   'Lettre à un militant algérien' (Letter to an Algerian Militant), *oc*, *iv*, 352.

6   Germaine Tillion, *France and Algeria: Complementary Enemies*, trans. Richard Howard (New York, 1961), p. 149.

7   Ahmed Taleb was writing in August 1959. See Agnès Spiquel and Philippe Vanney, Introduction to *Actuelles iii. Chroniques algériennes*, *oc*, *iv*, 1420.

8   Ibid., 1419.

9   Information drawn from Herbert R. Lottman, *Albert Camus: A Biography* [1979] (Corte Madera, *ca*, 1997), p. 657.

10 Mouloud Feraoun, 'La Source de nos communs malheurs' (The Source of Our Common Woes), *Preuves* (September 1958), reproduced in Feraoun, *L'Anniveraire* (Paris, 1972), pp. 35–44.

11 Ibid., pp. 36–7.

12 Ibid., pp. 37–8.

13 Ibid., pp. 38–9. The quotation from Camus begins: 'Kabyles are thus calling for schools just as they are calling for bread' (*oc*, *iv*, 323).

14 Feraoun, *L'Anniversaire*, p. 41.

15 Ibid., p 39.

16 Camus and Grenier, *Correspondance*, p. 222.

17 See Spiquel and Vanney, Introduction to *Actuelles iii*, *oc*, *iv*, p. 1407–8.

18 Camus writing from Le Panelier on 30 June 1947, Albert Camus and René Char, *Correspondance, 1946–1959*, ed. Franck Planeille (Paris, 2007), p. 25.

19 Ibid., p. 39.

20 Letter of 20 October 1952, Camus and Char, *Correspondance*, p. 101.

21 Albert Camus and Louis Guilloux, *Correspondance, 1945–1959*, ed. Agnès Spiquel-Courdille (Paris, 2013), p. 48.

22 September 1956 diary entry, *oc*, *iv*, 1253.

23 Postcard of 21 June 1958, Camus and Grenier, *Correspondance*, p. 218.

24 Camus and Char, *Correspondance*, p. 171.

25 See editor's note, Camus and Grenier, *Correspondance*, p. 272.

26 Camus and Char, *Correspondance*, editor's note 3, p. 25.

27 Camus and Guilloux, *Correspondance*, p. 58.

28 Camus and Char, *Correspondance*, p. 91, note 1.

15 Cohabiting with Oneself

1 Camus' last interview, *OC*, IV, 661.

2 Dostoyevsky refers to 'the so-called "progressives"', *The Devils*, trans. David Magarshack (London, 1971), p. 459.

3 See editorial note of Eugène Kouchkine, *OC*, IV, 1467.

4 Olivier Todd, *Albert Camus: une vie* (Paris, 1996), p. 732.

5 Letter to Carl Viggiani, 23 June 1959, quoted in Todd, *Albert Camus: une vie*, p. 728.

6 See Todd, *Albert Camus: une vie*, p. 753. See also Herbert R. Lottman, *Albert Camus: A Biography* [1979] (Corte Madera, CA, 1997), p. 674.

7 Albert Camus and René Char, *Correspondance, 1946–1959*, ed. Franck Planeille (Paris, 2007), p. 176.

8 Albert Camus and Jean Grenier, *Correspondance, 1932–1960*, ed. Marguerite Dobrenn (Paris, 1981), p. 226.

9 *FM*, 104; translation modified.

10 Todd, *Albert Camus: une vie*, p. 741.

11 *FM*, 253; translation modified.

12 Mouloud Feraoun, *L'Anniveraire* (Paris, 1972), p. 43.

13 Mohamed Lebjaoui, *Vérités sur la révolution algérienne* (Paris, 1970), pp. 48–9.

14 Max-Paul Fouchet, *Un jour, je m'en souviens* (Paris, 1968), p. 34.

15 Lottman, *Albert Camus*, pp. 686–7.

16 Feraoun, *L'Anniversaire*, p. 38.

17 See chapter Sixteen.

18 William Faulkner, *Requiem for a Nun* [1951] (London, 1961), p. 44.

19 Ibid., pp. 35, 89.

20 Ibid., p. 32.

21 Maurice-Edgar Coindreau's French translation of Faulkner's *Requiem for a Nun* appeared in 1957 with a preface by Camus.

22 Todd, *Albert Camus: une vie*, p. 744.

23 Quoted in Todd, *Albert Camus: une vie*, p. 744.

24 Lottman, *Albert Camus*, p. 691.

16 A Contested Legacy

1 Quoted in Julian Jackson, *France: The Dark Years, 1940–1944* (Oxford, 2001), p. 112.

2 Raymond Aron, *L'Opium des intellectuels* (Paris, 1955), p. 64.

3 A 1945 diary entry by Camus, quoted in Pierre-Louis Rey, *Camus, L'Homme révolté* (Paris, 2006), p. 91.

4 Albert Camus and René Char, *Correspondance, 1946–1959*, ed. Franck Planeille (Paris, 2007), p. 116.

5 Ibid., pp. 214–15.

6 Annie Cohen-Solal, 'Camus, Sartre et la guerre d'Algérie', in *Camus et la politique*, ed. Jeanyves Guérin (Paris, 1986), pp. 177–84 (p. 183).

7 Jean-Paul Sartre, *Situations*, IV (Paris, 1964), p. 126.

8 Ibid., p. 127.

9 *Hommage à Albert Camus 1913–1960, Nouvelle Revue française*, LXXXVII (March 1960), p. 403.

10 *Hommage à Albert Camus*, p. 538, italics in the original. The English version is here taken from Joseph Blotner, *Faulkner: A Biography* (London, 1974), vol. II, pp. 1756–7.

11 See Patrick McCarthy, *Camus* (New York, 1982), p. 323.

12 Jules Roy, *La Guerre d'Algérie* (Paris, 1960), p. 13.

13 Ibid., p. 14.

14 Ibid., pp. 208–9.

15 *Hommage à Albert Camus*, p. 440.

16 Broadcast of 19 June 1972. The Dib interview was one of six portraits of Camus in a series by Pierre Minet entitled 'Portraits' which was re-broadcast on 'Nuits', *France-Culture*, 26 December 2012.

17 Assia Djebar, *Le Blanc de l'Algérie* (Paris, 1995), p. 121.

18 See Patrick Crowley, 'Myth, Modernism, Violence and Form: An Interview with Salim Bachi', *Bulletin of Francophone Postcolonial Studies*, IV/1 (Spring 2013), pp. 2–11 (p. 9). Bachi's publications include a novel which draws on elements of Camus' life, *Le Dernier Eté d'un jeune homme* (The Last Summer of a Young Man) (Paris, 2013).

19 'Camus et moi, avec Benjamin Stora', *France-Culture* radio interview, 27 December 2012.

20 See above, chapter Six.

21 See, for example, Emily Apter, 'Out of Character: Camus's French Algerian Subjects', in E. Apter, *Continental Drift: From National Characters to Virtual Subjects* (Chicago, IL, and London, 1999), pp. 60–75.

22 'Mouloud Mammeri et la vision de l'Algérie de Camus', www.ina.fr, 1 August 2014.

23 E. Morin writing in *Autocritique* (Paris, 1975), p. 83; quoted by Maurice Weyemberg and Raymond Gay-Crosier in their editorial presentation of *L'Homme révolté*, OC, III, 1221.

24 Jean Daniel, *Avec Camus: Comment résister à l'air du temps* (Paris, 2006), pp. 88–9.

25 Maurice Merleau-Ponty, *Humanisme et Terreur: Essai sur le problème communiste* (Paris, 1947), p. 186; Jean Sénac, *Pour une terre possible . . . Poèmes et autres textes inédits* (Paris, 1999), p. 191.

26 Edward Said, *Culture and Imperialism* (London, 1994), p. 224.

27 Quoted in Benjamin Stora and Jean-Baptiste Péretié, *Camus brûlant* (Paris, 2013), pp. 83–4.

Select Bibiliography

Camus' Writings in French

Camus' complete works are available in the authoritative Gallimard
  (Pléiade) edition: Albert Camus, *Œuvres complètes*, 4 vols (Paris,
  2006–8), ed. Jacqueline Lévi-Valensi (vols I and II) and Raymond
  Gay-Crosier (vols III and IV). Many of Camus' works are also
  available in paperback in the Gallimard (Folio) collection.

A Selection of Works by Camus in English translation

Albert Camus: Lyrical and Critical, trans. Philip Thody (London, 1967)
American Journals, trans. Hugh Levick (London, 1989)
Between Hell and Reason, trans. Alexandre de Gramont (London, 1991)
Caligula & Three Other Plays (includes *The Misunderstanding, State of
  Siege, The Just Assassins*), trans. Stuart Gilbert, with a preface by
  Justin O'Brien (New York, 1962)
Camus at 'Combat': Writing, 1944–1947, ed. Jacqueline Lévi-Valensi,
  trans. Arthur Goldhammer, with a foreword by David Carroll
  (Princeton, NJ, 2006)
Exile and the Kingdom, trans. and afterword, Carol Cosman
  (London, 2006)
The Fall, trans. Robin Buss (London, 2013)
The First Man, trans. David Hapgood (London, 1995)
A Happy Death, trans. Richard Howard [1973] (London, 2002)
Lyrical and Critical Essays, trans. Ellen Conroy Kennedy (New York, 1967)
The Myth of Sisyphus, trans. Justin O'Brien, with an afterword by James
  Wood (London, 2013)
Notebooks I: 1935–1942, trans. Philip Thody (New York, 1963)

Notebooks II: 1942–1951, trans. Justin O'Brien [1965] (New York, 1995)
Notebooks, 1951–1959, trans. Ryan Bloom (Chicago, IL, 2008)
The Outsider, trans. Sandra Smith (London, 2012); also available as
     The Stranger, trans. Matthew Ward (New York, 1988)
The Plague, trans. Robin Buss, with an introduction by Tony Judt (London,
     2002)
The Rebel, trans. Anthony Bower, with an afterword by Olivier Todd
     (London, 2000)
Resistance, Rebellion, and Death, a selection of Camus' interventions in
     public debate, trans. Justin O'Brien (London, 1961)
Selected Political Writings, ed. and trans. Jonathan H. King (London, 1981)
Youthful Writings, trans. Ellen Conroy Kennedy (New York, 1976)

Camus' Correspondence

Camus, Albert, and René Char, *Correspondance, 1946–1959*, ed. Franck
     Planeille (Paris, 2007)
Camus, Albert, and Jean Grenier, *Correspondance, 1932–1960*,
     ed. Marguerite Dobrenn (Paris, 1981)
Camus, Albert, and Louis Guilloux, *Correspondance, 1945–1959*,
     ed. Agnès Spiquel-Courdille (Paris, 2013)
Camus, Albert, and Pascal Pia, *Correspondance, 1939–1947*,
     ed. Yves-Marc Ajchenbaum (Paris, 2000)
Camus, Albert, and Francis Ponge, *Correspondance, 1941–1957*,
     ed. Jean-Marie Gleize (Paris, 2013)

Biographical Works on Camus

Doudet, Sophie, Marcelle Mahasela, Pierre-Louis Rey, Agnès Spiquel
     and Maurice Weyembergh, *Albert Camus: Citoyen du monde*
     (Paris, 2013)
Lottman, Herbert R., *Albert Camus: A Biography* [1979] (Corte Madera,
     CA, 1997)
Todd, Olivier, *Albert Camus: une vie* (Paris, 1996); as *Albert Camus: A Life*
     (abridged), trans. Benjamin Ivry (London, 1997)

A Select Bibliography of Works on Camus

Abbou, André, *Albert Camus entre les lignes: Adieu à la littérature ou fausse sortie? 1955–1959* (Biarritz, 2009)

Achour, Christiane, *Un Etranger si familier: Lecture du récit d'Albert Camus* (Algiers, 1984)

Apter, Emily, 'Out of Character: Camus's French Algerian Subjects', in E. Apter, *Continental Drift: From National Characters to Virtual Subjects* (Chicago, IL, and London, 1999)

Aronson, Ronald, *Camus and Sartre: The Story of a Friendship and the Quarrel that Ended It* (Chicago, IL, and London, 2004)

Bachi, Salim, *Le Dernier Eté d'un jeune homme* (Paris, 2013)

Banks, G. V., *Camus: 'L'Etranger'* (Glasgow, 1992)

Bishop, Tom, and Coralie Girard, eds, *Camus Now* (*The Florence Gould Lectures at New York University*, vol. XII, Winter 2010–11)

Braun, Lev, *Witness of Decline: Albert Camus, Moralist of the Absurd* (Rutherford, NJ, 1974)

Bronner, Stephen Eric, *Camus: Portrait of a Moralist* (London, 1999)

Carroll, David, *Albert Camus the Algerian: Colonialism, Terrorism, Justice* (New York, 2007)

Chaulet-Achour, Christiane, and Jean-Claude Xuereb, eds, *Albert Camus et les écritures algériennes: Quelles Traces?* (Cahors, 2004)

Cohen-Solal, Annie, 'Camus, Sartre et la guerre d'Algérie', in *Camus et la politique*, ed. Jeanyves Guérin (Paris, 1986), pp. 177–84

Cruickshank, John, *Albert Camus and the Literature of Revolt* (New York, 1960)

Cruise O'Brien, Conor, *Camus* [1970] (London, 1982)

Daniel, Jean, *Avec Camus: Comment résister à l'air du temps* (Paris, 2006)

Dunwoodie, Peter, *Une histoire ambivalente: Le dialogue Camus-Dostoïevski*, with a preface by Ernest Sturm (Paris, 1996)

Ellison, David, *Understanding Albert Camus* (Columbia, SC, 1990)

Fitch, Brian T., *The Narcissistic Text: A Reading of Camus's Fiction* (Toronto, 1982)

Foley, John, *Albert Camus: From the Absurd to Revolt* (Stocksfield, Northumbria, 2008)

Foxlee, Neil, *Albert Camus's 'The New Mediterranean Culture': A Text and its Contexts* (Bern, 2010)

Gonzales, Jean-Jacques, *Albert Camus: L'Exil absolu* (Houilles, 2007)

Grenier, Jean, *Albert Camus souvenirs* (Paris, 1968)

Grenier, Roger, *Albert Camus. Soleil et ombre: Une biographie intellectuelle* (Paris, 1987)

—, ed., *Album Camus* (Paris, 1982)

Guérin, Jeanyves, *Camus: Portrait de l'artiste en citoyen* (Paris, 1993)

—, ed., *Camus et la politique* (Paris, 1986)

—, ed., *Dictionnaire Albert Camus* (Paris, 2009)

Haddour, Azzedine, 'The Camus-Sartre Debate and the Colonial Question in Algeria', in *Francophone Postcolonial Studies: A Critical Introduction*, ed. Charles Forsdick and David Murphy (London, 2003), pp. 66–76

Hommage à Albert Camus 1913–1960, *Nouvelle Revue française*, LXXXVII (March 1960)

Hughes, Edward J., *Albert Camus: 'Le Premier Homme', 'La Peste'* (Glasgow, 1995)

—, ed., *The Cambridge Companion to Camus* (Cambridge, 2007)

Isaac, Jeffrey C., *Arendt, Camus and Modern Rebellion* (London, 1992)

Judt, Tony, *The Burden of Responsibility: Blum, Camus, Aron and the French Twentieth Century* (Chicago, IL, and London, 1998)

King, Adele, ed., *Camus's 'L'Etranger': Fifty Years On* (New York, 1992)

Lévi-Valensi, Jacqueline, and André Abbou, eds, *Fragments d'un combat 1938–1940: Alger Républicain/Le Soir Républicain* (Cahiers Albert Camus 3), 2 vols (Paris, 1978)

McCarthy, Patrick, *Camus* (New York, 1982)

—, *Camus: 'The Stranger'* (Cambridge, 2004)

Margerrison, Christine, *'Ces Forces obscures de l'âme': Women, Race and Origins in the Writings of Albert Camus* (Amsterdam, 2008)

Margerrison, Christine, Mark Orme and Lissa Lincoln, eds, *Albert Camus in the 21st Century: A Reassessment of his Thinking at the Dawn of the New Millennium* (Amsterdam, 2008)

Moreau, Jean-Luc, *Camus l'intouchable* (Montreal, 2010)

Morisi, Eve, ed., *Albert Camus contre la peine de mort*, with an essay by E. Morisi and preface by Robert Badinter (Paris, 2011)

Onfray, Michel, *L'Ordre libertaire: La vie philosophique d'Albert Camus* (Paris, 2012)

Orme, Mark, *The Development of Albert Camus's Concern for Social and Political Justice* (Cranbury, NJ, 2007)

Rey, Pierre-Louis, *Camus: L'Homme révolté* (Paris, 2006)

Showalter, Jr, English, *Exiles and Strangers: A Reading of Camus's 'Exile and the Kingdom'* (Columbus, OH, 1984)

Sprintzen, David, *Camus: A Critical Examination* (Philadelphia, PA, 1988)

Stora, Benjamin, and Jean-Baptiste Péretié, *Camus brûlant* (Paris, 2013)

Thody, Philip, *Albert Camus* (London, 1989)

Walker, David, ed., *Albert Camus: Les Extrêmes et l'équilibre: Actes du colloque de Keele, 25–27 mars 1993* (Amsterdam, 1994)

Weyembergh, Maurice, *Albert Camus, ou la mémoire des origines* (Brussels, 1998)

Williams, James S., *Camus: 'La Peste'* (London, 2000)

Zaretsky, Robert, *A Life Worth Living: Albert Camus and the Quest for Meaning* (Cambridge, MA, 2013)

Acknowledgements

I wish to record my considerable thanks to the Leverhulme Trust for generously awarding me a one-year Research Fellowship which enabled me to take this project forward and to Queen Mary, University of London, for granting me a term's leave to ensure completion of the book. Sincere thanks also go to Vivian Constantinopoulos at Reaktion Books for her guidance throughout and to Amy Salter in her role as text editor.

In writing the book, I have benefitted greatly from the support and advice of colleagues. Charles Forsdick, Susan Harrow and Eric Robertson offered invaluable help at numerous stages and it is a pleasure to record my gratitude to them. I have also profited a great deal from discussions about Camus with Peter Dunwoodie, Raymond Gay-Crosier, Peter Hallward, Libby Saxton, Andreas Schönle, Michael Sheringham, David Walker and James Williams. Thanks are also due to Adrian Armstrong, Cynthia Gamble, José Lenzini, John Lyons, Gabriel Naughton, Mark Smith and Adam Watt and, for their kind provision of reading material, to Yves Bodot and Nathalie Crouzet.

Finally, in thanking my family, I want to record in particular my indebtedness to Kathleen for her unfailing help and great patience.

Photo Acknowledgements

The author and the publishers wish to express their thanks to the below sources of illustrative material and /or permission to reproduce it:

Archives Municipales de la Ville de Saint-Étienne: p. 181; photo by H. Bertault reproduced in Antoine Chollier, *Alger et sa région* (Grenoble, 1929), courtesy of the Bibliothèque Nationale de France: p. 53; photo by H. Bertault reproduced in Antoine Chollier, *Alger et sa région* (Grenoble, 1929), courtesy of the Bibliothèque Nationale de France: p. 33, photo by H. Bertault reproduced in Antoine Chollier, *Alger et sa région* (Grenoble, 1929), courtesy of the Bibliothèque Nationale de France: p. 142; courtesy of the Bibliothèque Nationale de France: p. 21; Corbis: p. 8 (Condé Nast Archive); Département des Estampes et de la Photographie, Bibliothèque Nationale de France: pp. 13, 38, 50, 51, 52; courtesy Editions Gallimard: pp. 71, 132; Fotostiftung Schweiz, Winterthur: p. 121; Gamma-Rapho/Keystone: pp. 127, 135; photo by A. Jouve reproduced in Henry de Montherlant, *Il y a encore des paradis: Images d'Alger 1928–1931* (Algiers, 1935), courtesy of the Bibliothèque Nationale de France: p. 41; courtesy *La Marseillaise*: p. 159; © *Nouvelle Revue française*: p. 181; Photo OFALAC (Tourist Board of the Government General of Colonial Algeria), reproduced in Henry de Montherlant, *Il y a encore des paradis: Images d'Alger 1928–1931* (Algiers, 1935), courtesy of the Bibliothèque Nationale de France: p. 167; Rex Shutterstock: pp. 42 (Roger-Viollet), 88 (Mémorial Leclerc – Musée Jean Moulin / Roger-Viollet), 101 (Universal History Archive / Universal Images Group), 124 (Sipa Press), 136 (Roger-Viollet), 141 (Roger-Viollet), 145 (Sipa Press), 184 (Roger-Viollet).